A Guide to Curriculum Planning in Driver and Traffic Safety Education

Randall R. Thiel, Ph.D.
Consultant
Alcohol and Traffic Safety

Wisconsin Department of Public Instruction
Madison, Wisconsin

This publication is available from:

Publication Sales
Wisconsin Department of Public Instruction
Drawer 179
Milwaukee, Wisconsin 53293-0179
(800) 243-8782

Bulletin No. 96300

© 1996 Wisconsin Department of Public Instruction

ISBN 1-57337-029-0

The Wisconsin Department of Public Instruction does not discriminate on the basis of sex, race, religion, age, national origin, ancestry, creed, pregnancy, marital or parental status, sexual orientation, or physical, mental, emotional or learning disability.

Printed on recycled paper.

Contents of the Guide

	Page
Foreword	v
Acknowledgments	vii

1 Introduction
Purpose of the Guide	2
Special Features	2
Outline	3
Background	3
References	8

2 Administration of Driver and Traffic Safety Education Programs
Program Standards	10
Scheduling	13
Program Equity	14
Instructor Issues	15
Administration of Laboratory Instruction	16
Program Assessment	23
References	25

3 Instruction
Introduction	28
Instructional Topics	35
Instructional Considerations: Simulation	80
Instructional Considerations: On-Street Driving Instruction	82
Instructional Considerations: Range	86
References	90

4 Integration with School and Community
Integration within Curriculum	92
Integration with Other Health Programs	93
Integration Beyond the Classroom	96
References	103

5 Issues and Trends
Outside Contracting	106
Instructor Shortages	107
Graduated Licensing	107
Advancements in Technology	109
References	110

6 Appendixes
A. PI 21 of the Wisconsin Administrative Code	112
B. PI 3.13 of the Wisconsin Administrative Code	116
C. Resources	117

Foreword

Ensuring the health and safety of students is an important part of the educational mission. Nowhere does this mission have greater relevance than in driver and traffic safety education.

Automobiles and the highway transportation system help citizens lead active, productive lives. But such benefits are not without their costs. Unfortunately, automobiles and other vehicles have the potential to cause injuries, take lives, damage property, and harm the natural environment. Strong educational programs are one way to limit these costs.

The state legislature recognizes the value of traffic safety education and offers financial support, in the form of state driver education categorical aid reimbursements, to traffic safety programs. Educators of this state have also invested a great deal of time and energy in Wisconsin's traffic safety education program. Through the work of consultants to the Department of Public Instruction, previous publications, and contributions by educators statewide in state and national professional traffic safety associations, Wisconsin has developed a national reputation for its strong support of driver education.

This publication will aid the continued support of traffic safety programs and the vital mission of helping young citizens pursue safe and healthy transportation. I am sure I am not alone among the citizens of Wisconsin in extending my heartfelt appreciation to all of those who work to keep the roadways and young citizens of this state safe.

John T. Benson
State Superintendent of Public Instruction

Acknowledgments

Contributors

A Guide to Curriculum Planning in Driver and Traffic Safety Education was developed with the generous assistance of many individuals and organizations. Among those deserving of thanks are the following:

Members of the Driver Education Curriculum Advisory Committee

David Burg
Driver Education Teacher
Brillion High School

Francis Eckerman
Concerned Citizen and
  Former Traffic Safety Specialist

Thomas Hercules
Principal
Hustisford High School

Carol Karsten
Alcohol Countermeasurer Program
  Manager
Wisconsin Department of Transportation

David Knutson
Driver Education Teacher and Former
  President
Wisconsin Driver and Traffic Safety
  Education Association

Mark Nelson
Representative
Wisconsin School Safety Coordinator's
  Association

Robert Wing
Former Traffic Safety Coordinator
Madison Metropolitan School District

Members of the Driver Education Curriculum Advisory Writing Committee

Susan Abing
Driver Education Teacher
Potosi High School

James Giese
Driver Education Teacher
Medford High School

Chuck Johnson
Driver Education Coordinator
Milwaukee Public Schools

Paul Koski
Driver Education and Tech. Prep. Teacher
Menasha High School

Mike McGinley
President, Wisconsin Driver and Traffic
  Safety Education Association
Driver Education Teacher
Oshkosh North High School

Jeanie Medema
Driver Education Teacher
Germantown High School

Neal Rathjen
Former Driver Education Coordinator
Milwaukee Public Schools and
Representative, Wisconsin Driver and
  Traffic Safety Education Association

Mike Shucha
Driver Education Teacher
Waunakee High School

Al Stevens
Driver Education Teacher
Tomah High School

Bob Warren
Driver Education Teacher
Kenosha Tremper High School

Thanks are also due to past, present, and future driver and traffic safety educators for helping to make Wisconsin a national leader in ensuring the health and safety of novice drivers.

Staff Contributors

Division for Learning Support: Equity and Advocacy

Student Services Prevention and Wellness Mission Team Members deserve thanks for their efforts toward improving the lives of students through promotion of prevention and wellness efforts.

Juanita S. Pawlisch, Ph.D.
Assistant Superintendent

Nancy F. Holloway, Director
Divisionwide Policy and Human Resources

Michael Thompson, Team Leader
Student Services, Prevention, and Wellness Team

Division for Libraries and Community Learning

Publications Team
Brian Lavendel, Editor
Victoria Horn, Graphic Artist
Neldine Nichols, Photographer
Dianne Penman and Gail Endres, Typesetters
Jessica Early, Proofreader

Thanks are also due to Margaret T. Dwyer and Brian Satrom, Editors, for editorial advice, and to Jane Grinde, Director of the Bureau for School and Community Relations, for support and coordination.

Copyrighted Materials

Every effort has been made to ascertain proper ownership of copyrighted materials, to credit original authors, and to obtain permission for use where necessary. Any omission is unintentional.

Introduction 1

Purpose of the Guide
Special Features
Outline
Background
References

Wisconsin's first state curriculum guide, *Man, Vehicle and Environment* (1970), was considered one of the best driver and traffic safety education guides in the country. That resource, combined with sustained legislative and financial support from the state, and the work of dedicated traffic safety education professionals statewide, has helped Wisconsin develop one of the best traffic safety programs in the country. This guide is intended to continue that tradition.

Purpose of the Guide

This publication will be useful for those who plan, revise, administer, or carry out traffic safety education in the public high schools of Wisconsin. This guide will also serve as a resource for
- teachers and administrators of teacher preparation programs and of non-public driver education programs,
- teachers-in-training, and
- curriculum planners.

Program administrators will find this publication helpful for its thorough treatment of administrative concerns. Instructors will find this guide useful for its information on course objectives, topics, content, and student activities, much of which was developed with the aid of driver and traffic safety educators statewide.

Special Features

The guide was written with the understanding that programs are most successful when local school districts develop a curriculum to suit local needs. Wisconsin does not have a state mandated curriculum or textbook adoption requirement. This guide is meant to facilitate, rather than to mandate, curriculum planning at the local level.

Although Wisconsin's public high school driver education courses have a great deal of consistency in content, some differences can be seen in
- amount of classroom instruction,
- types and amount of laboratory instruction,
- whether credit goes toward satisfying graduation requirements,
- whether driver education is an elective or required class,
- student fees,
- scheduling,
- contractual arrangements,
- vehicle acquisition, and
- accessibility to various driving environments.

This curriculum guide is distinctive in that it combines the curriculum content from all instructional phases, such as classroom, simulator, multiple-vehicle range, and on-street driving instruction. Thus the curriculum planner or instructor can choose the content, instructional method, and timing most appropriate to local needs. A great deal of the instructional portion of this guide is a direct result of contributions of driver and traffic safety education teachers from across the state.

Driver and traffic safety education is adapting to new and diverse methods of instruction. This guide presents a variety of instructional methodologies and activities to encourage teachers to incorporate a wide range of teaching practices.

Outline

This guide is organized into the following chapters: introduction, administration, instruction, integration with school and community, and issues and trends.

The chapter on administration discusses administrative elements of driver education programs. It includes program approval standards, a discussion of various instructional formats—with administrative issues faced under specific phases, and scheduling considerations.

The chapter on instruction presents general beliefs about teaching traffic safety education, an introduction to a variety of instructional strategies, and an extensive list of instructional topics, including objectives, content, and student activities.

The chapter on integration with school and community notes the significant impact factors outside the driver education program, such as peers, other classes, family, and the community at large, have on student driving behaviors.

The final chapter looks ahead to anticipate some of the issues and trends driver and traffic safety education faces now and will face in the future.

Background

The Need for Driver and Traffic Safety Education

Driver and traffic safety education evolved from a recognition that education is essential to the development of safe motor vehicle operators. More than 50 years ago, state policy makers worked to make driver education a part of the public school curriculum. In 1938, Madison was the first Wisconsin school district to offer classroom and laboratory driver instruction. Today, hundreds of school districts throughout the state offer driver education.

Most citizens are dependent on the highway transportation system each and every day of their lives. Those who operate vehicles on the roadways have a responsibility to do so safely, efficiently, and responsibly. But such a complex system is not hazard free; each year traffic crashes result in thousands of deaths and injuries nationwide. Young people tend to be more affected than others by the risks of driving or being a passenger. A glance at the following recent statistical evidence supports this.

Most citizens are dependent on the highway transportation system.

- Young drivers are overrepresented in traffic deaths nationwide; those under 21 years of age comprise 7.7 percent of all licensed drivers yet account for 18 percent of drivers involved in traffic crashes that result in a death (National Safety Council, 1991). Young drivers comprise 7 percent of the total driving population yet are involved in 13 percent of all alcohol-related crashes (National Highway Traffic Safety Administration, 1994).
- Wisconsin licensed drivers age 16 to 20 comprised 7.6 percent of all licensed drivers in the state yet represented 15.6 percent of all the drivers that were involved in a crash (Wisconsin Department of Transportation, 1991).
- Wisconsin drivers under the age of 20 were involved in an injury or fatality crash an average of once every 50.3 minutes in 1990 (WDOT, 1991).
- The crash rate per mile for drivers age 15 to 20 is about four times that of adults (NHTSA, 1994).
- Forty-one percent of all deaths involving 15 to 20 year olds are the direct result of motor vehicle crashes (Department of Public Instruction, 1994).
- Of all drivers, young drivers use safety belts the least (Liberty Mutual, 1992).

Crashes not only cost lives, they cost money.

The data support the premise that young drivers are overrepresented in traffic crashes. The NHTSA (1994) suggests that reasons for this include "lack of driving experience, lack of adequate driving skills, excessive driving during nighttime high-risk hours, risk-taking, and poor judgement and decision-making skills."

Clearly, efforts to provide novice drivers instruction in traffic safety should continue. If it is agreed that "health promotion, youth development, and prevention of risk behaviors should be an integral part of a school's approach to education," as noted in the *Framework for an Integrated Approach to Student Services, Prevention, and Wellness Programs* (DPI, 1995), then traffic safety education is an essential component of the curriculum.

Economic Considerations

Crashes not only cost lives, they cost money. According to the National Safety Council (1995), the average nationwide costs of traffic collisions were estimated as follows:
- each motor vehicle-related death $920,000
- nonfatal disabling injury $ 34,200
- property damage crash (including minor injury) $ 6,600

Based on these estimates, the cost of Wisconsin's traffic-related fatalities was approximately $650 million in 1994. Statewide costs for the 103,934 property damage crashes were about $686 million (WDOT, 1994). Given that traffic crashes cause significant economic loss in addition to painful personal loss, driver education programs may be a cost efficient means of reducing those losses. Yet many driver and traffic safety education programs have been faced with severe budgetary threats. Many programs have been reduced to minimum length, while others have eliminated portions of instructional content. Today, many teachers and administrators are forced to defend traffic safety programs from cutbacks or, in some cases, elimination.

Though most cutbacks are a result of local budgetary constraints, some critics attempt to justify reductions or eliminations based on the premise that driver education is not as effective as it should be. But driver and traffic safety education cannot be expected to serve as a panacea for unsafe driving behaviors; driver educators, parents, school board members, and government officials must understand that there are limits to what driver education alone can be expected to achieve.

While driver education can play an important role in the development and preparation of young drivers, it is only one of many factors influencing the preparation of novice drivers. The Foundation for Traffic Safety of the American Automobile Association (AAA) (1995) agrees that driver education alone is not the answer to a safe highway transportation system. Formal instruction alone cannot be expected to develop safe and responsible drivers. Driver education programs need support from other components of the curriculum, and from student services, peer groups, families, and society at large. At the same time, driver education instructors must work closely with others, such as parents, community organizations, and other safety partners. Driver education alone has not, nor will it, guarantee safe drivers. Still, driver education plays an important role in preparing novice drivers. Driver education may be the only formal instruction in traffic safety some students will ever receive. As such, driver and traffic safety education deserves continued and significant support from all stakeholders.

Basic Beliefs

This guide is based on the following beliefs about students, schools, driving, teaching and learning, and the role of driver and traffic safety education.
- Users of the highway transportation system need to be educated to use it safely, effectively, and efficiently.
- High school driver education offers a formal and consistent program of instruction to a vast majority of the population reaching driving age.
- Traffic safety education involves not only learning how to operate a motor vehicle, but also the development of safe, responsible driving skills.
- Driving is both a mental and a physical process; safe driving requires instruction and experience in using mental faculties.
- Driver education programs are integral to local districts' alcohol and other drug abuse education and prevention and wellness program.
- Driver education is a small investment to minimize death, injury, and property loss resulting from crashes.
- Adult-supervised practice and the gradual granting of driving privileges help develop safer, more experienced drivers.
- Strong parental and community support exists for high quality traffic safety education.
- Schools have a vested interest in students' health and an obligation to discourage youth participation in high risk behavior.
- High school driver education instructors are often deeply involved in their schools and have a genuine interest in the health and well being of their students and communities.

These "basic beliefs" provide direction for the mission and purpose of programs in driver and traffic safety education.

Mission of Wisconsin High School Driver and Traffic Safety Education

With the passage of the 1966 Highway Safety Act, states received federal highway safety program funds. A portion of these funds was used for driver education programs. States were charged with developing and implementing a uniform program of instruction for students reaching licensing age.

Driver and traffic safety education is...a critical life long skill affecting the conservation and quality of human health and life.

The mission of driver education in Wisconsin high schools is to provide students with skills to drive safely. Driver and traffic safety education is based on the belief that this is a critical life long skill affecting the conservation and quality of human health and life. In order to accomplish its mission, driver and traffic safety education programs focus on providing learning opportunities for the development of the skills, knowledge, and thought processes necessary to become a safe and efficient driver, and a responsible user of the Highway Transportation System (HTS).

The Automotive Safety Foundation (1970) published a traffic safety education curriculum resource guide listing three aims of driver education. Those aims remain as valid today as when they were published. Those aims are

- to prepare students with at least minimum capabilities for entry into the highway traffic system as vehicle operators,
- to equip students with the knowledge and thought processes to enable them to make wise decisions as drivers, and
- to help students acquire the insight and motivation needed to become responsible users of the highway transportation system.

The general goal of driver and traffic safety education, according to the foundation, is "to improve the quality of human decisions and performance tasks related to the system in a manner that encourages continuing improvement."

Achieving the Goals of Driver and Traffic Safety Education

All Wisconsin public school districts are charged with helping students meet prescribed goals and outcomes, as noted in Wisconsin *Learner Goals, Outcomes, and Assessment: Educating Students for Success in the 21st Century* (DPI, 1994). Student performance outcomes provide a basis upon which districts can develop assessments to determine the effectiveness of an educational program. Objectives provide instructors with direction as to what content to teach and what students should be learning. At the same time, performance outcomes provide students with an understanding of what will be expected of them. As with any other subject, driver and traffic safety instruction should support those outcomes. Objectives should be relevant, measurable, and clearly stated. Through such objectives, students should be able to understand

- the knowledge or skill they are expected to know or to do,
- the conditions under which they will be expected to conduct the assigned task,
- the criteria by which they will be evaluated, and
- what constitutes an acceptable performance.

Wisconsin Learner Goals and Outcomes

Wisconsin learner goals state that the learner will
- build a substantial knowledge base,
- develop thinking and communication processes,
- apply knowledge and processes,
- acquire the capacity and motivation for life long learning,
- develop physical and emotional wellness,
- develop character,
- be a responsible citizen,
- be prepared for productive work,
- respect cultural diversity and pluralism, and
- develop aesthetic awareness.

These goals are reflected in learner outcomes that state that students should be capable of the following skills:
- Identify, develop, evaluate, and apply criteria to ideas, products, or performance of oneself or others.
- Revise a product, performance, system, or idea in response to relevant information.
- Make informed decisions by examining alternatives and anticipating consequences of actions.
- Achieve desired results by interpreting and executing instructions, plans, models, and diagrams.
- Recognize and devise systems and describe their interdependence.
- Create a quality product, process, or performance that will meet a need.
- Respond to the aesthetic, intellectual, and emotional aspects of an event, performance, or product.
- Transfer learning from one context to another.
- Recognize, define, and solve a problem.
- Recognize and communicate one's strategies for accomplishing objectives.
- Work effectively in groups to accomplish a goal.
- Defend a position by integrating information from multiple sources.
- Develop and test a hypothesis.
- Recognize when a need for specific information exists and demonstrate the ability to locate, evaluate, and focus that information.
- Conceive of places, times, and conditions different from one's own.
- Identify compelling personal interests and goals and pursue them.
- Recognize the influence of diverse cultural perspectives on human thought and behavior.

Applying Learner Goals and Outcomes to Driver and Traffic Safety Education

Wisconsin's learner goals can be applied to driver education programs. Driver education instructors can expect that students will
- build a substantial knowledge base of traffic safety information,
- develop thinking and communication processes,
- apply knowledge and processes,
- develop safe driving behaviors,
- be responsible traffic citizens,
- realize and appreciate that driving privileges facilitate increased mobility that may lead to greater job opportunities,
- respect and appreciate other highway users, and
- appreciate the significant role the highway transportation system plays in their own lives and society.

In order to realize these outcomes, instructional plans must identify objectives, content, and student activities to promote learning for all students.

References

AAA Foundation for Traffic Safety. *Novice Driver Education Model Curriculum Outline*. Washington, DC, 1995.

Automotive Safety Foundation. *A Resource Curriculum in Driver and Traffic Safety Education*. Washington, DC: Automotive Safety Fdtn., 1970.

Liberty Mutual Insurance Group. *Teen Driving Fact Sheet* (Pub. No.: PR 138 B). Liberty Mutual Insurance Group, 1992.

National Highway Traffic Safety Administration. *State Legislative Fact Sheet: Graduated Driver Licensing System*. Washington, DC, Sep., 1994.

National Safety Council. *Accident Facts*. 1991 ed. Chicago: National Safety Council, 1991.

_____. *Accident Facts*. 1995 ed. Itasca, IL: National Safety Council, 1995.

Wisconsin Department of Public Instruction. *Framework for an Integrated Approach to Student Services, Prevention, and Wellness Programs*. Madison: DPI, 1995.

_____. *Man, Vehicle and Environment*. Madison: DPI, 1970.

_____. *Wisconsin Learner Goals, Outcomes, and Assessment: Educating Students for Success in the 21st Century*. Madison: DPI, 1994.

_____. *Youth Risk Behavior Survey Results*. Madison: DPI, 1994.

Wisconsin Department of Transportation. *1991 Wisconsin Traffic Crash Facts*. Madison: WDOT, 1991.

_____. *1994 Wisconsin Traffic Crash Facts*. Madison: WDOT, 1994.

Administration of Driver and Traffic Safety Education Programs

Program Standards
Scheduling
Program Equity
Instructor Issues
Administration of Laboratory Instruction
Program Assessment
References

The organization and operation of quality driver and traffic safety education requires skillful and professional management by school administrators. The distinctive features of the classroom and laboratory phases of driver and traffic safety education require the cooperation and participation of many different agencies, organizations, and individuals. Program administrators must be aware of standards required for program approval. This chapter addresses those standards and a wide range of related administrative issues.

Program Standards

The DPI is charged with approving and administering high school driver education programs in both public and private high school settings. To carry out this responsibility, the DPI developed program standards as set forth in PI 21 of the Wisconsin Administrative Code (Wis. Adm. Code) (see appendix A). These rules establish minimum standards for program approval, standards for the issuance of course completion certificates, requirements for categorical aid eligibility, and uniform vehicle marking standards for driver education vehicles.

Program Terminology

Local program administrators should be familiar with terminology used in PI 21, Wis. Adm. Code, and elsewhere. Following are definitions of some of the more common terms.

Approved Driver Education Program is a complete course of instruction including at least 30 clock-hours of classroom instruction and six hours of on-street driving—or its equivalent if adequate amounts of simulation and/or multiple-vehicle range instruction is provided.

Behind-the-Wheel Instruction is that portion of the driver education program in which a student actually drives a vehicle. It includes multiple-vehicle range as well as on-street driving.

Block Program refers to a driver education program in which a specific phase of the program must be successfully completed before the student advances to the next phase. This should not be confused with school-wide block scheduling, in which fewer but longer classes are held.

CESA is an acronym for "cooperative educational service agency." CESAs, of which there are 12 in Wisconsin, provide educational support services to school districts.

CHCEB refers to county handicapped children's education boards. For more information on these, refer to ch. 115 of the Wisconsin Statutes.

Concurrent Programs are programs in which two or more phases of instruction are provided to students at the same time.

Laboratory Instruction is the portion of a driver education program that provides students with driving experiences, including on-street, range, observation, and simulation instruction.

Multiple-Vehicle Driving Range Instruction takes place when students drive a vehicle at an off-street driving facility on which a number of motor vehicles operate simultaneously.

Observation Instruction occurs when students are passengers in a vehicle in which another student is receiving behind-the-wheel instruction. Observation instruction can include on-street and multiple-vehicle range observation.

On-Street Instruction refers to instruction received by a student when the student drives a vehicle on public streets or highways in a dual-controlled vehicle under the supervision of a driver education teacher, or when the student is a passenger in the vehicle while another student is driving.

Simulation Instruction is instruction obtained through the use of synthetic training devices.

TC is an acronym for technical college.

Approved Programs

An approved public or private high school program meets or exceeds the minimum requirements of the program standards as established by the DPI. These standards are defined in PI 21, Wis. Adm. Code. Program approval is required if a public or private high school is to receive course completion certificates and if public schools are to be eligible for state driver education categorical aid reimbursement.

Local program administrators are required to submit applications for program approval to the DPI annually. The reports are reviewed to ensure that the program satisfies standards of PI 21, Wis. Adm. Code. After the review is complete, local program administrators are informed of the results.

Approved programs are eligible to receive student course completion certificates (form PI 1714) for students who successfully complete the program. Local program administrators may request certificates using an "application for driver education course completion certificates" (form PI 1715). Course completion certificates should be issued only to students who successfully complete an approved program of instruction. Issued certificates are used by the WDOT to verify that the student has completed an approved program and, if between 16 and 18 years of age, is eligible to take the driver's license exam. Copies of issued course completion certificates are to be kept by the school and may be used to verify requests for driver education categorical aid reimbursement.

Course Approval Standards

PI 21, Wis. Adm. Code, also states requirements programs must meet in order to receive DPI approval. State statutes define approved driver education programs for those under the age of 18 as
- public or private high schools that meet the minimum standards as established by the DPI,

- technical colleges that have been approved by the Technical College Board, and
- commercial driving schools that have been approved by the WDOT to teach students under the age of 18.

Approved programs are those that include at least 30 clock-hours of classroom instruction, six hours of in-car observation, and six hours of on-street, behind-the-wheel instruction. Simulation and multiple-vehicle range instruction may be substituted for a portion of the on-street driving according to guidelines as set forth in PI 21, Wis. Adm. Code.

The classroom portion of a driver education program offered during the school year must extend over a minimum of six weeks, whereas summer classroom programs may last as few as three weeks.

In cases when more than 13 months elapse between the time classroom instruction ends and in-car, on-street driving instruction begins for any student, a ten-hour refresher classroom course must be provided.

Driver Education Categorical Aids

Approved public school driver education programs qualify for state categorical aid.

Approved public school driver education programs qualify for state categorical aid reimbursement for driver education. The DPI pays districts up to a maximum of $100 per student who successfully completes an approved program of driver education. Payments are based on annual program reports. The number of students claimed on the annual report should correspond to the number of course completion certificates issued by the district during the preceding fiscal year.

Student Fees

Local school districts are authorized to assess student fees for any part of a driver education program, provided that portion of the program is not required for graduation and does not provide credit toward graduation. According to recent data, 70 percent of public school programs charged student fees in the $26 to $150 range. The average fee of all public high school programs is approximately $65 to $70 per student.

When setting student fee rates, administrators should strive to keep fees low enough that the cost is not prohibitive for families with tight budgets. Fortunately, despite fiscal constraints, most districts have been able to offer driver education programs at reasonable costs, and thereby provide instruction to all eligible students in their communities.

Wisconsin Driver Education Certificates

Driver education programs are required to report to the DPI the number of students who successfully complete the program. In order for a student to successfully complete a classroom program of instruction, the student must have received a passing grade and have participated in at least 30 hours of classroom instruction. (Thus, merely participating in instruction does not assure the student of successfully completing the classroom phase. Determination of successful completion is left to the district.)

The department provides programs with driver education course completion certificates, which are issued to each student who successfully completes the approved program.

These certificates show that the student has successfully completed an approved program, and, if the student is at least 16 years old, makes them eligible to apply for a Wisconsin driver's license. Successful completion is achieved when the student receives a passing grade in the course and participates in at least the minimum hours of instruction as set forth in PI 21, Wis. Adm. Code.

If local credit is awarded, students may not be failed for poor course attendance alone. Therefore, local programs that award credit need to establish procedures for students to make up missed work.

Program Records

Approved programs of instruction are required to maintain copies of their program approval forms (PI 1709) for a period of at least seven years. Copies of course completion certificates (PI 1714), or the newer certificate stubs, should be kept for a minimum of five years. All other student records should be kept according to other state or local policy.

Every program should maintain records of in-car, on-street driving instruction for each student. These records should include basic information, including the student's legal name, address, and phone number; instruction permit number; dates and amounts of driving; observation time awarded; and descriptions of instructional content.

Uniform Vehicle Markings

PI 21, Wis. Adm. Code, states requirements that driver education vehicles must meet if they are to be used for on-street driving instruction. Instructors and program administrators should review the actual language as set forth in PI 21, Wis. Adm. Code (see appendix A).

Scheduling

Driver education programs are affected by scheduling of the school day and by scheduling of the driver education program itself. For example, some schools have moved toward "block scheduling," in which classes are scheduled for longer periods over shorter terms. The shift toward block scheduling creates unique situations for driver education. For example, although many schools conduct on-street driving instruction outside of normal school hours, those that schedule it during the class day will have to make adjustments under block scheduling. In some cases, driver education is paired with another course, and the two courses are scheduled on opposite days during the term.

Some driver education programs are conducted outside of the normal school day or during the summer. When programs are offered during such times, administrators are advised to limit classroom instruction to no more than two hours per day. Scheduling driver education outside of normal school hours can potentially limit student access, as families may have difficulty arranging transportation or adapting their schedules. Another potential disadvantage to summer scheduling is that summer programs tend to include fewer classroom hours due to attempts to adapt the driver and traffic safety education curriculum to the tight schedules of summer school. Obviously, reducing the number of hours of instruction can have a detrimental effect on the quality of instruction.

Traffic safety classes should also have class size limits.

Current data from driver and traffic safety education programs in Wisconsin show that
- 11 percent of driver and traffic safety education programs are summer-only programs,
- 32 percent of the schools offer driver education during the school year only,
- 50 percent of the schools offer driver education during both the school year and the summer, and
- 6 percent do not offer driver education.

When arranging schedules, administrators also need to be aware of the effect class size has on the quality of instruction. Just as core subject areas have class size limits, traffic safety classes should also have class size limits. Classes that are too large restrict the instructor's ability to engage students and to manage the class.

Program Equity

Over the past three decades, significant progress has been made in ensuring the educational rights of students with exceptional education needs (EEN). Legislation has been enacted that requires local school districts to ensure that no student is discriminated against. Districts are required, where appropriate, to ensure that educational services be in place for students with identified conditions, for example, physical handicap, mental or developmental disability, hearing handicap, visual handicap, speech or language handicap, emotional disturbance, or learning disability.

In districts offering driver education, instruction must be made available to all eligible students, regardless of handicap. If it is determined that a local program cannot adequately accommodate a student's special educational needs or services, it is the responsibility of the district to ensure that the student is provided a separate but equal alternative program that provides the specific instruction or special service. When alternative programs or services are provided, they should be provided with as few restrictions, disruptions, differences, or inconveniences to the student as possible.

Most local districts have developed systematic ways of having district staff, including school guidance counselors, psychologists, and special education staff, communicate with driver education instructors in advance so that appropriate instruction can be provided, often with the assistance of Multidisciplinary Teams (or "M-Teams"). M-Teams identify students with special needs and plan collaborative efforts to ensure that students are provided equal educational opportunities. Through the efforts of the M-Team, individual education plans are developed to determine special education services needed for the student.

Though most EEN students can participate in the classroom portion of a driver education program, some students require rather extensive adaptive equipment in order to participate in on-street instruction. In such cases, districts are advised to seek assistance from an outside agency or organization which has the necessary equipment. Special contractual arrangements can be made for such services.

Instructors and program administrators are encouraged to contact the DPI's Exceptional Education Needs Team or Alcohol Traffic Safety Consultant (see appendix C) to discuss special educational needs.

Instructor Issues

Essential to any quality program of instruction is the availability of qualified and dedicated instructors. This section addresses DPI requirements for driver education certification, trends in instructor availability and certification, and program options for delivering instruction. These requirements can be found in PI 3.13, Wis. Adm. Code (see appendix B).

Instructor Certification Requirements

Instructors of approved programs must be employees of the district, CESA, TC, or CHCEB that is providing the instruction. Individuals who teach in approved public or private high school programs (or those public school programs that are contracted out to CESAs or TCs) are required to hold a driver education teaching license through the DPI. Individuals who are licensed as commercial driving school instructors only may not be used as instructors in approved public school programs. Private school programs, or CESAs and TCs that are contracted to provide driver education instruction for public schools, must also use DPI-licensed driver education teachers, and the instructors must be employees of their organizations.

Driver education certification requires that teachers complete an instructional program consisting of 15 semester credits in prescribed coursework, including
- basic driver education,
- advanced driver education,
- basic safety,
- alcohol and other drugs, and
- behavioral aspects of crash prevention.

In addition to completing an approved instructor preparation program, all driver education instructors are required to have an acceptable driving record. The WDOT monitors driving records of driver education instructors and reports those records to the DPI. Unacceptable records can lead to suspension or revocation of teacher certification.

All DPI-certified driver education instructors must renew their certifications every five years. This can be accomplished by taking approved courses at approved colleges, universities, and technical colleges. Recertification can also be accomplished by attending DPI-approved conferences or workshops in order to obtain equivalency clock hours. Currently, 30 equivalency clock hours can be substituted for one semester of college credit.

Instructor Availability

Currently there are over 900 instructors teaching in 388 approved public school driver education programs in Wisconsin. Approximately two-thirds of these instructors are employed on a part-time basis; most of them teach on-street driving.

Recently, many districts have faced a shortage of driver education instructors. These shortages may be due to increased teacher retirements. Because a large portion of driver education instructors are nearing retirement, programs are likely to face a potential shortage of driver education teachers in the future. This shortage has been made more severe by a reduction in the number of colleges and universities offering driver education teacher certification programs. Currently only two institutions in Wisconsin (UW–Whitewater and UW–Stout) continue to offer such programs. Meanwhile, the number of college students taking traffic safety education courses and completing certification programs as undergraduates has dropped. Most of those completing certification programs currently hold teaching positions in other disciplines and seek driver education certification to increase their job security or earning power.

Administrators in need of additional driver education instructors should consider elementary teachers as a pool of potential instructors. Numerous elementary teachers are certified in driver education and those who are not need only complete the required coursework.

Administration of Laboratory Instruction

Laboratory instruction, as defined by PI 21, Wis. Adm. Code, is that portion of a program that provides students driving experiences. It includes behind-the-wheel instruction, observation instruction, and simulation instruction. A comprehensive program of driver and traffic safety education includes instruction in both classroom and laboratory instruction. Approved programs are required to offer at least six hours of observation instruction and six hours of behind-the-wheel, on-street driving instruction. Programs that use simulation or multiple-vehicle range are allowed to reduce the number of hours of behind-the-wheel, on-street driving according to rules set forth in PI 21, Wis. Adm. Code.

Administrators and instructors need to be aware of program standards that govern the laboratory phases. This section discusses laboratory instruction guidelines and suggestions.

On-Street Driving

On-street driving is a critical component of any approved driver and traffic safety education program. It is during this phase that students use the classroom and laboratory skills they have acquired.

Definitions and Standards

On-street driving instruction takes place when a student drives a vehicle on public streets or highways in a dual-controlled vehicle under the supervision of a driver education teacher, or when the student is a passenger in the vehicle while another student is driving. Though sometimes referred to as behind-the-wheel (BTW) instruction, administrative rules define BTW instruction as "that portion of the driver education program in which the student is actually driving a vehicle." Thus, on-street driving and multiple-vehicle range instruction both qualify as BTW instruction.

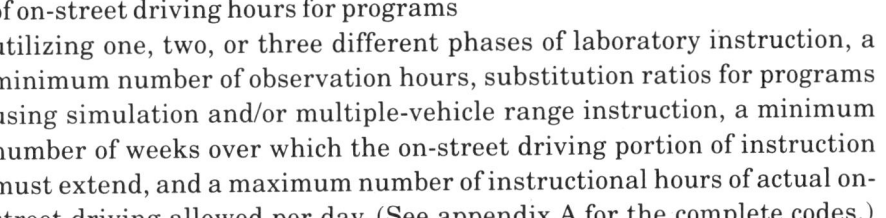

There are several standards relevant to the on-street driving phase of a driver education program; these standards are contained in PI 21, Wis. Adm. Code. The codes require uniform vehicle markings, a minimum number of on-street driving hours for programs utilizing one, two, or three different phases of laboratory instruction, a minimum number of observation hours, substitution ratios for programs using simulation and/or multiple-vehicle range instruction, a minimum number of weeks over which the on-street driving portion of instruction must extend, and a maximum number of instructional hours of actual on-street driving allowed per day. (See appendix A for the complete codes.)

On-street driving is a WDOT requirement for individuals under the age of 18 who wish to apply for their driver's license prior to their eighteenth birthday. State statutes require that a minimum of six hours of on-street instruction be completed, although, as previously mentioned, simulation and/or range instruction can substitute for a portion of the on-street instruction.

In-car observation is also required for individuals under the age of 18. A minimum of six hours of in-car observation is required. Range observation is permitted and carries an equivalency ratio of one to one. Thus, a student who was provided six hours of range driving and four hours of in-car range observation would also need at least two hours of in-car, on-street observation.

On-street driving must extend over a minimum of three full school weeks. In addition, no student may receive more than one hour of on-street driving instruction per day. The scheduling requirements are based on the belief that shorter on-street lessons offered over a longer period of time offer students greater opportunity to learn than longer lessons over a shorter period of time. Also, shorter and more frequent instruction extends the period of time over which students can obtain practice driving outside of class.

All on-street instruction provided in a DPI-approved program must be conducted in a dual-controlled vehicle, with a DPI-licensed and certified driver education teacher occupying the front passenger seat. Up to three students may sit in the back seat. Wisconsin requires the use of occupant restraints for all passengers. Driver education programs using vans are also required to limit the number of total occupants to five people.

Equipment and Supplies

Driver education vehicles used for on-street driving instruction are required to be properly marked as described in PI 21, Wis. Adm. Code. Vehicles must have a functioning dual-controlled brake. In addition, all driver education vehicles must be insured and licensed. Vehicles licensed with driver education plates may be used for providing on-street driving instruction only. Vehicles not licensed with driver education plates may be used if they are also used for other purposes.

Though standards do not require it, the following items should be kept in vehicles used for on-street instruction:
- an instructor's inside rear-view mirror;
- an accident report form;
- a fire extinguisher;
- student record forms;
- an instructor clipboard, note pad, or binder;
- supplemental instructional materials, such as diagrams of intersections; and
- a camera.

Acquisition of Vehicles

Vehicle acquisition is a crucial administrative responsibility. Program administrators and instructors need to be aware of alternatives for obtaining vehicles. Although in the past, vehicles were often loaned to driver education programs free of charge, today many dealers negotiate lease or rental agreements with local schools.

Public school driver and traffic safety education programs have several options for obtaining vehicles. Some common ways to obtain vehicles include
- lease arrangements—often used for programs that extend over longer periods of time, such as a semester or school year;
- rental arrangements—daily rental fee more appropriate for shorter programs, such as a summer-only program;
- free loan—when available;
- district purchase of a new vehicle;
- district purchase of a used vehicle—some programs purchase vehicles from car rental companies; and

- temporary loan vehicle from a local dealer—upon return of the vehicle the dealer sells the vehicle, with the local district paying the difference between the original and actual sales price.

Whatever option is used, districts will benefit from maintaining good relationships with local dealers. Administrators having difficulty obtaining a vehicle for their program can contact the Automobile and Truck Dealers Association (see appendix C).

Simulation

Simulation has special administrative considerations. In Wisconsin, in the 1995-96 fiscal year, 90 public school programs (nearly one-quarter of all programs) provided simulation instruction. The following portion of the guide addresses administrative concerns specific to programs utilizing simulation instruction.

Definitions and Standards

Administrative rules define simulation instruction as "the use of synthetic training devices to prepare a student for driving a real motor vehicle." According to *The Driving Simulator Method* (Highway Users Federation for Safety and Mobility, 1970), the driving simulator method of instruction involves student interaction with filmed driving environments.

Simulation can be substituted for on-street driving based on a four to one ratio. Thus, four hours of simulation instruction can substitute for one hour of on-street driving—provided that each student receives at least three hours of actual on-street driving instruction. If multiple-vehicle range instruction is used to supplement classroom, simulation, and on-street driving, up to four hours of the total six-hour requirement can be satisfied through the combination of range and simulation instruction.

Advantages

A number of advantages result from the incorporation of simulation into a program's laboratory offerings. Some of the major advantages are that simulation provides
- a low risk instructional environment,
- instruction in diverse driving environments and weather conditions within a relatively short period of time for all students,
- practice with visual perception skills,
- cost efficient pupil-teacher ratios, and
- accessible learning experiences for students who are physically challenged.

Types of Simulation Installations

Simulation installations commonly found in public school driver education programs may be permanent or portable. Most simulators offered to districts through CESAs are portable. A number of schools have simulator units permanently installed. In other instances, districts have incorporated portable classrooms and have installed simulator installations in these semi-permanent facilities separate from the main school building.

Acquisition of Simulation Equipment

Because of the initial expenses associated with purchasing simulation equipment, many districts may find it advantageous to consider alternatives. Simulation equipment can be purchased, rented, leased, or contracted through CESAs. A number of Wisconsin districts rent simulation equipment. In some instances, the services of an instructor are included in the rental fee.

When the simulation system is rented from a CESA, the simulator is transported from school to school. Scheduling needs to be considered, however, as districts must accommodate the CESA schedule. For example, during the brief time that the simulator is available, special scheduling arrangements may be necessary.

In some instances, districts enter into a lease-to-purchase agreement with the equipment manufacturer. The district pays a specified amount over a period of months, and upon completion of the contract, the simulator becomes the property of the district. Some districts have explored cooperative agreements whereby the costs of a portable simulation installation is shared among them, and the equipment is transported within the sharing districts. Thus, several districts benefit and significant costs savings can be realized.

Districts opting to purchase simulation equipment need to plan ahead for a variety of issues. Simulation equipment will need to be serviced on a regular basis. As with any equipment, simulator units encounter periodic problems. In addition, districts will need to maintain a film library.

Multiple-Vehicle Range

The number of high school driver education programs offering multiple-vehicle range instruction has declined over the years. Due to increased vehicle cost and difficulty in establishing a facility, fewer programs utilize multiple-vehicle range instruction.

Multiple-vehicle range programs were analyzed in the 1960s to evaluate the effectiveness of multiple-vehicle range instruction. The early studies (for example, Nolan, 1964; Gustafson, 1965) examined driving records of young drivers who received range instruction in their high school driver education programs. The records of these students were compared to those of drivers who did not receive range instruction. Findings indicated that driving records between the two groups did not differ significantly. As a result, range instruction substitution standards were established, allowing local driver education programs to reduce the actual amount of on-street driving instruction by substituting range instruction based on a two to one ratio. As an added benefit, range instruction also provided a significant cost savings to large programs—at least until the price of fuel increased and free loan vehicles became less common.

Currently, fewer than 15 public school programs in Wisconsin offer multiple-vehicle range instruction. Most of the programs offering multiple-vehicle range instruction do so in the summer only due to the difficulty of locating an adequate facility.

A number of items need to be considered in determining whether to incorporate range instruction into an existing program. Some of these items include
- the number of students enrolled in the driver education program and potential cost savings over on-street instruction only,
- the number of vehicles available for use on the range, and
- the availability of space, the location, and the size of the facility.

Multiple-vehicle ranges can provide instruction in mixed traffic environments, specific skill exercises, emergency exercises, or advanced driving skills.

Definitions and Standards

PI 21, Wis. Adm. Code, defines multiple-vehicle range as a "designated off-street facility on which a number of motor vehicles operate simultaneously during instruction under the supervision of one or more teachers who are positioned outside the vehicle." Aaron and Strasser (1977) describe a multiple-vehicle driving range as "an off-street driving area designed to incorporate a variety of realistic traffic situations where a number of vehicles are used simultaneously, under the supervision of one or more instructors" to develop driver skills.

Districts offering multiple-vehicle range instruction for the first time are required to contact the DPI so that an on-site review can be conducted. In addition, technical support can be provided by the department.

Though no specific Wisconsin Administrative Codes apply to the maximum number of hours of range instruction any student may receive per day, administrators are encouraged to limit the amount of range driving instruction to a maximum of one hour per day. Range instruction is not to be counted in the three week minimum time period over which on-street driving must extend.

Advantages

In range instruction, more cars than teachers function simultaneously and students are instructed by a teacher positioned outside the vehicle. Because of these characteristics, multiple-vehicle range instruction provides real-life learning opportunities for students. Such an environment requires students to utilize decision making skills and to independently respond to situations, rather than simply be told what to do.

In contrast to on-street driving, multiple-vehicle ranges provide a learning environment that emphasizes the development of manipulative skills. Multiple-vehicle facilities not only have two-way and one-way streets to simulate traffic flow, they provide students with ample opportunity to develop their manipulative skills. In addition, students can gain more concentrated practice executing specific driving exercises than in on-street driving.

Though it may appear that because there is no teacher in the vehicle, the range method has higher levels of risk than the in-car instruction method, students develop a high degree of self-reliance and independent decision making skills. Furthermore, levels of risk can be reduced by
- thoroughly orienting students to the range and each range lesson,
- designing the facility and locating skill exercises for increased safety,
- utilizing a communications system through which every vehicle can clearly hear instructor directions, and
- utilizing well trained instructors.

Although range instruction can offer efficient student-to-teacher ratios, for safe and well supervised instruction, programs should not exceed a 12 to one vehicle-to-teacher ratio.

Equipment Supplies and Facility Characteristics

There are two types of multiple-vehicle range facilities: dedicated facilities and shared facilities. Very few schools continue to have ranges that are only used for instructional purposes. Most programs utilize a parking lot that, when not in use as a range, serves as a parking facility.

The availability of vehicles is a major administrative aspect to consider. Because few automobile dealers provide vehicles on a free loan basis, many districts cannot afford the number of vehicles necessary to realize significant cost savings.

The availability of space and the location of the facility need to be considered. It is recommend that the minimum size of a range facility be 200 feet by 400 feet, and that the site have the following characteristics:
- ample space for the development of basic skills
- road surfaces wide enough for two-way traffic flows
- properly marked intersections and curves
- standard lane markings and signs, and in some cases signals

A well designed range facility should also allow for an instructor's unobstructed view of the entire facility, incorporate an adequate communications system, and be designed with the needs of the students in mind. The most widely used multiple-vehicle range resource, *The Multiple Car Method* (Automotive Safety Foundation, 1967), states that specific functions are important to consider when planning a range layout. Some of the considerations include
- standard road markings
- standard highway signs
- operational traffic light, if possible
- a perimeter roadway with two lanes 12 feet wide
- cross roads—including a major four-way intersection and T-intersections
- a straight section of road for simulated passing
- inclusion of a T-exercise
- inclusion of an X-exercise
- areas for angle parking and parallel parking (ideally on both sides of the street to simulate one-way and two-way streets)

- inclusion of a Y-exercise for turnabouts
- inclusion of a double garage exercise
- one-way and two-way streets

Though range instruction has been on the decline, it has been found to be an effective and cost efficient instructional approach, especially for large programs.

Program Assessment

Background

Program assessments are essential in determining the value of educational programs. Despite the fact that nearly every driver education program undergoes a program review as part of a district's academic accreditation review process, ongoing local assessment will ensure that high quality is maintained. Indeed, assessment is essential to the development and continued improvement of quality driver education programs. This section addresses assessment-related activities that can help driver education program planners maintain the best possible program given local needs, resources, and constraints. When conducted with the goal of improving programs and instruction, assessment and evaluation become the means whereby the continued quality of programs can be ensured.

Assessments vary from case to case and are conducted for a wide variety of reasons. The results of an assessment may, for example, be used to determine whether to implement a new program or to make modifications to an existing program. One of the overriding questions of any existing program assessment is whether the program adequately meets the required standards. If a district wishes to be eligible for driver education categorical aids, this is a prerequisite. Categorical aids notwithstanding, however, quality of programming should be a major goal in any program of instruction.

Assessment Considerations

One of the most important program components to assess is the curriculum. Ongoing assessment of curriculum can help determine whether changes are needed. As always, planners need to be aware of local needs while striving for optimum program quality given those local factors. Every program should have a formal, written curriculum with clearly stated objectives. These objectives, in turn, should serve as the guide for program content and instruction.

Assessment can also be used to evaluate whether the program is keeping pace with changes in the field. Some questions administrators may want to consider include the following: Is the program content current? Are students provided instruction in the latest technological and mechanical innovations in automotive or highway engineering? Does the curriculum reflect up-to-date laws? Are instructional resources, such as simulators, films, videos, and other instructional aids, current? Are program instructors taking part in regular, ongoing training and development in the field?

The instruction itself is another component that should be assessed. Assessment ought to help instructors and administrators provide an environment and use instructional strategies conducive to learning for all students. An assessment of educational strategies can pose the following questions: Are a variety of instructional strategies incorporated into the classroom phase of a driver education program? Are they the most appropriate strategies? And are they effective? Those assessing an educational program need to consider what instructional strategies are most effective for a specific topic or content area. For example, it would be more appropriate to have students engage in problem solving situations rather than rely solely on lectures in order to help students develop problem solving skills.

Instruction itself... should be assessed.

Another component worth reviewing is student assessment. How are students assessed in the driver education program? What must students know or be able to do in order to successfully complete the program? What criteria are used in the evaluation of students? What type of assessments are used to evaluate student knowledge and skill levels? Do assessment and test results actually measure those objectives? Are alternative assessments offered for those with special needs?

It may also be useful to assess certain administrative-related items. For example, changes in scheduling may have an impact on program effectiveness. In such cases, local instructors need to assess the potential impact of changes on instructional quality. The number of students in the program should also be examined. Any program has a maximum number of students which it can accommodate. Factors relevant to program capacity include the following:

- size of the target population
- number of qualified instructors
- number of vehicles
- program scheduling
- number of program instructional hours
- term over which instruction is provided

Programs should also seek feedback from parents and students—especially former students who have since obtained their driver's license, and have gained driving experience. These students will be able to provide invaluable feedback as to whether the program adequately met their needs as driver education students.

One should also assess local policies and practices. Examples may include review of

- student enrollment eligibility criteria for driver education
- local policies regarding home-schooled students' eligibility for enrolling in driver education
- how special needs students are provided program accessibility and instruction

- local attendance requirements for driver education, as compared to state law regarding attendance and failure situations
- fees charged to students
- extent to which the program meets or exceeds minimum standards

If programs of instruction are to continue to develop and to maintain quality, assessment and evaluation processes are essential.

References

Aaron, James E., and Marland K. Strasser. *Driver and Traffic Safety Education.* 2nd ed. New York: Macmillan, 1977.

Automotive Safety Foundation. *The Multiple Car Method.* Washington, DC: Automotive Safety Fdtn., 1967.

Gustafson, Robert E. "A Study to Compare the Effectiveness of Instruction in the Allstate Good Driver Trainer and on the Multiple-Car Off-Street Driving Range with the Multiple-Car Off-Street Driving Range." Diss. Michigan State Univ., 1965.

Highway Users Federation for Safety and Mobility. *The Driving Simulator Method.* Washington, DC: Highway Users Fedn. for Safety and Mobility, 1970.

Nolan, Robert O. "A Comparative Study of the Teaching of the Multiple-Car Off-Street Driving Range and the Aetna Drivotrainer." Diss. Michigan State Univ., 1964.

Instruction 3

Introduction
Instructional Topics
Instructional Considerations: Simulation
Instructional Considerations: On-Street Driving Instruction
Instructional Considerations: Range
References

Introduction

This chapter will be useful to curriculum developers and planners, and to teachers in the classroom and laboratory phases in which they teach driver and traffic safety education. This chapter includes discussion of the beliefs and goals of driver and traffic safety instruction. It also includes instructional methods teachers can use as they plan their instructional approach to driver and traffic safety education. This chapter concludes with an extensive collection of instructional topics, objectives, content, and activities intended to serve as resources for the development of a local driver and traffic safety education curriculum.

Goals

Underlying driver and traffic safety education programs are major program goals. The program goals set forth by the Automotive Safety Foundation (1970)—and which were introduced in chapter 1—are as follows:
- to prepare students with at least minimum capabilities for entry into the highway traffic system as vehicle operators,
- to equip students with the knowledge and thought processes to enable them to make wise decisions as drivers, and
- to help students acquire the insight and motivation needed to become responsible users of the HTS.

The driver education curriculum must grow out of these program goals; those involved in curriculum development should ensure that their programs are based on these program goals.

Optimum learning takes place when students are provided with a variety of learning experiences.

Instructional Methods

This section is based on the belief that optimum learning takes place when students are provided with a variety of learning experiences through different instructional methods, and when students are actively engaged in the learning process, supported with guidance and reinforcement, and allowed to learn from each other.

Traffic safety educators can take advantage of a wide variety of instructional methods. As teachers develop or revise instructional approaches, however, it will be helpful to remember that instruction can be made more effective through
- diverse instructional methods,
- active engagement of students, and
- content that is relevant to students' lives.

Instructors should recognize that all students do not learn equally well through any single instructional method. Engaging students in the learning process is an important instructional goal because students learn most effectively when they are active in the learning process. Use of an inquiry approach, for example, may lead to more complete integration of content than a more passive instructional method. It is also important that driver and traffic safety instructors make clear to students how instructional content is related to students' lives and to their future as responsible drivers. Following is a discussion of several instructional methods that can be applied in the driver education classroom.

Lecture

Direct oral presentation is often the most expedient way to relay information to a large number of students at one time. However, the lecture can restrict discussion or student inquiry due to time constraints and the one-way nature of the lecture as a mode of communication.

Because students will not be able to take notes on everything the instructor says, the instructor should consider providing handouts with an outline of the lecture. To maintain students' interest, instructors can use visual aids. For example, driving procedures for specific car maneuvers can be illustrated with the use of a traffic board or chalk board.

Topics suitable for lecture include procedures to obtain forms and signatures necessary for a permit or license, steps of specific driving exercises, summaries of drunk driving laws and penalties, or other important state traffic laws. In order to accommodate different learners, instructors should consider making an audio tape or video tape of the lecture for students with special needs.

Discussion

When properly facilitated, discussions provide students the opportunity to ask questions; seek clarification; or share their own thoughts, beliefs, or reactions to questions or concepts. Discussion must be managed to prevent a single individual—including the instructor—or group of individuals from monopolizing the discussion. The teacher's role is to facilitate open discussion.

■ Sample Activity

Discussion

1. Prepare a summary of the graduated licensing program.
2. Give each student a copy to review at home with a parent or guardian.
3. Facilitate a class discussion to elicit students' responses to questions such as: Why do you think this program is being considered? What components of the program do you feel will have the greatest potential impact for reducing motor vehicle crashes for young drivers? How might graduated licensing affect employment opportunities for young people, personal and family schedules, or involvement of students and families in extra-curricular programs? Inquire as to how students' parents react to graduated licensing. Were they receptive to the idea? What did they like and dislike about the program?

Depending on the size of the class, instructors may choose to limit students' responses to ensure that many students have the opportunity to contribute to the discussion. If a topic or issue meriting further discussion should arise, record it on a flip chart or on the board so it can be discussed at a later time or during another class session.

Problem Solving

The problem solving method of instruction gives students the opportunity to apply knowledge or feelings to specific problems. Problem solving can involve the integration of subject matter across the curriculum. For example, students can integrate mathematics and driver education to calculate a vehicle's total stopping distances at various speeds, or to calculate a vehicle's fuel efficiency based on the number of miles traveled and gallons of gas consumed.

■ Sample Activity

Problem Solving

Ask students to use their knowledge of mathematics to solve the following problems:

1. If a vehicle that gets 21 miles per gallon is driven 163 miles, how many gallons of fuel are used? Calculate to the nearest tenth of a gallon.

2. If the average price of gas is $1.13 per gallon, how much would it cost to purchase 8.7 gallons of gas?

3. How might one calculate the average highway fuel efficiency (in miles per gallon) for a vehicle that has just under a half-tank of fuel?

4. Two vehicles are traveling toward each other from opposite directions. They are exactly three miles apart. One is traveling at 45 mph and the other is traveling at 50 mph. How long will it take for the two vehicles to meet?

5. If the speedometer indicates that a vehicle is traveling 107 km/h (kilometers per hour), what is its speed in miles per hour?

6. An increase in the speed limit may increase the earnings of some. For example, a truck driver can drive a maximum of eight hours on any given day. She's on the road six days a week, 48 weeks a year. At a rate of pay of $0.275 a mile, how much more money will she be able to make over one year at speeds of 65 mph as opposed to 55 mph?

On the other hand, higher speeds often correlate with increased numbers of crashes. If the increased speed limit caused a 6 percent increase in the number of fatalities, how many more people would die annually in the state of Wisconsin, where 706 people were killed in 1994?

Small Group Work

Groups of students can be asked to discuss issues and to come to group consensus regarding a controversy. Examples might include having small groups develop a group consensus on the following issues: graduated licensing for novice drivers, drinking age, penalty differences for younger and older drivers, mandatory helmet law, photo radar, media messages regarding alcohol consumption, and so on.

■ Sample Activity

Small Group Work

Ask small groups to plan a trip. In preparation for this activity, identify various destinations and ask the groups to do the following:

1. Identify the shortest route between the school and their destination. Identify the route to be traveled and the number of miles to be traveled on each roadway.

2. Assign each group a vehicle with a specific fuel mileage. Have each group calculate the total number of miles they will travel to reach their destination, calculate the amount of fuel needed for the trip, and, using an average local cost per gallon of gas, determine the cost of the fuel.

3. Have the students calculate the total cost and duration of the one-way trip assigned to their group using data such as the cost of meals, overnight accommodation, speed limits, rest stops, maximum mileage per day, and so on.

Reaction Statements

A provocative way to stimulate discussion, reaction statements provide an opportunity for discussion of controversial issues. A reaction statement is a statement designed to elicit reaction from students. It is important that the instructor facilitate the discussion to ensure that all views are aired and given consideration.

Individual Reports or Projects

Asking students to compose reports or projects provides an opportunity to integrate writing into the driver and traffic safety education classroom. This technique allows students to explore topics of personal interest and topics that warrant extended research beyond class time.

Development of Student Traffic Safety Groups

Many schools use the driver education classroom to start such groups as Students Against Driving Drunk (SADD) chapters or peer helpers. Many students who take driver education classes may never again receive a formal program of instruction in traffic safety, but a youth traffic safety group can provide a means for local driver educators to work with students throughout their high school careers.

Videos or Films

Since driving is largely based on visual senses, audiovisual materials are an excellent way to enhance classroom instruction. In order to enhance the instructional value of audiovisual aids and other media, the material should be integrated into the classroom through discussion and other activities. When selecting materials, instructors need to ensure that materials do not present mixed messages (especially relating to underage drinking or drinking and driving).

Case Studies of Accident Reports

Students have the opportunity to use an inquiry approach, in which students are encouraged to discover information and solutions on their own, as they review accident reports to identify causative factors and driver actions that might have avoided collision. Students could also try to categorize the major causative factor as operator, vehicle, or environment.

Guest Speakers

Many driver education classes utilize guest speakers. The guest speaker should be an authority on the subject. Instructors should encourage the speaker to focus the presentation on information that is useful and interesting to the students. The speaker should avoid mixed messages that conflict with safe driving behaviors.

Homework Assignments

Homework gives students an opportunity to work on subject matter for which there may be insufficient time in class. Programs with minimal hours of classroom instruction can use homework to ensure that students are provided learning opportunities on content not covered within the regular confines of the classroom. However, homework must be integrated into the class. This might necessitate that instructors take a few moments in class to review homework and discuss students' work.

Use of Traffic Safety Articles

Articles on traffic safety issues published in newspapers, magazines, and, in some cases, traffic safety research can supplement material presented in class. Research provides articles on such topics as vehicles, legislation, programs, and traffic safety issues in general.

Role Play

Role playing consists of carefully planned and prescribed situations to involve students and to provide an opportunity for students to develop critical observation and listening skills. After role playing is complete, students can discuss actions, situations, and statements from the role playing situation. Students can then analyze and critique the situations and actions observed. Finally, students can discuss alternative courses of action that might be used in a similar, real-life situation.

■ Sample Activity

Role Play

Three students role play a situation in which they are "hanging out" in a restaurant parking lot after a big game. It's nearly 10:00 p.m. and one of the students needs to go home, as she is scheduled to take an exam the next morning. (She had planned to get a good night's sleep in order to prepare for the test.) Friends drive up in another car and report that a big party—at which alcohol will likely be served—is being held at a classmate's home. The three discuss whether to go. The student who has the test is pressured by the other two to attend the party. The test-taker, who is a passenger in another student's car, lives in the opposite direction of the party site. The driver, wanting to go to the party, assures the passenger that she will be taken home before her parents return.

1. Have students role play a scenario in which the student eventually gives in and goes along.

2. After the role play, ask a volunteer to incorporate refusal skills and attempt to gracefully decline the invitation. The scenario could be discussed in class, or another student could be given the opportunity to try refusing with dignity.

Games

Learning can be fun. When properly planned and conducted, games are a valuable strategy for improving motivation and learning.

■ Sample Activity

Games

Select a game format that most students are familiar with and develop traffic safety questions around specific categories. Categories might include traffic laws, driving procedures, terminology, car trivia, roadway sign recognition, universal symbols, alcohol laws and penalties, perceptual skills, traffic safety organizations, or problem solving. Develop questions and award points based on responses. Different levels of questions and points can be awarded depending on the difficulty of the questions. Explain rules and time limits for responses. Instructors may choose to offer rewards or incentives.

Peer Education

The active involvement of students in preparing and conducting presentations for other students is an effective form of learning. Peer education groups are used in schools nationwide for a wide variety of subjects. Many districts have peer educators who lead activities in alcohol and other drug abuse programs. SADD is one example of a very successful organization that emphasizes the empowerment of youth in addressing various issues around prevention education.

Peer education can be conducted at same-age levels or at cross-age levels. Classroom instructors can incorporate peer education into driver education courses by asking driver education students to make presentations to elementary school students. Students can be assigned topics and activities to research, plan, and present. This format encourages students to take a more active role in the class, and it also encourages students to take on increased levels of responsibility.

■ Sample Activity

Peer Education

Divide the class into groups (four to five students per group). Assign each group a major traffic safety topic area. Examples might include child safety seats and how to use them properly, general occupant safety restraints, alcohol and traffic safety, risky driving behaviors, pedestrian safety, or bicycle safety. Have students prepare a lesson, including activities and exercises appropriate for the particular grade level. Groups can also video tape the presentations for review purposes. Assess the presentations and allow groups to modify their presentations. Encourage using different media (computer-generated presentations, self-produced home videos, slides, transparencies, and so forth). Develop criteria upon which their presentations will be evaluated, including minimum and maximum time limits. Later, groups can be assigned to present to other classes. If the presentations are to be made to a different grade level, instructors can seek assistance from those teachers or district staff.

Field Trips or On-Site Visits

Though field trips are rare in many districts, trips to a business, agency, or organization can be both a valued learning experience for students and an excellent public relations technique for a driver education program.

■ Sample Activity

> **Field Trips or On-Site Visits**
>
> Identify a local automotive dealership (perhaps one that is involved in your driver education program) having both a sales and a service department. Bring students to the dealership for a guided informational tour. Before the tour, develop a mutual understanding with the tour guides as to what items or areas might be most valuable to the students.

Instructional Topics

This section contains information developed by driver and traffic safety education instructors throughout Wisconsin. Though local programs differ in terms of when they are offered, the number of phases that are offered, and the number of hours of instruction provided, the following topics can be adapted to local needs.

Introduction

This collection of instructional topics is not a curriculum in itself, but is intended as a resource for local curriculum planning. Districts may wish to use this section for suggested topics, but specific decisions involving course syllabi or specific lesson plans are best made at the local level. This material is offered with the expectation that instructors and administrators will make their own decisions about what material to present in their own programs and how to present it. Teachers and administrators thus retain flexibility for their programs and for how local programs are arranged.

How to Use this Section

Readers will note that the following instructional topics are presented in no particular order—neither chronological nor by suggested emphasis. Some instructional topics that follow may be better suited to one phase of instruction (classroom, simulation, or behind-the-wheel instruction) than another. At the same time, there is overlap between topics and phases of instruction. Various topics and content can be integrated throughout instruction. Of course, instructors should determine which phase is most appropriate for teaching a given topic. Instructors in minimum length programs need to be very selective in determining what content is covered in which phase of their program. Teachers must adjust their time frames to their own local needs and to the amount of class time available. These determinations are left to local decision makers. Such curriculum development is an ongoing process; administrators and instructors need to consider new information and alternative instructional methods on an ongoing basis.

Most of the following topics are presented in three sections—objectives, content, and student activities. The "objectives" section identifies suggested objectives (or outcomes) for each instructional topic. One way to measure the success of the teaching and learning program is to assess whether students are able to fulfill the stated objectives. These objectives can become performance indicators, should local programs desire. Teachers and administrators are encouraged to develop their own objectives and means for assessing the success of their instructional programs. Explicit objectives help students understand and gain the knowledge and skills being taught. For further discussion of assessment issues, refer to chapter 2 of this guide.

The "content" section identifies material related to each instructional topic. The content items are not exhaustive nor required. The examples provided offer local planners the opportunity to compare their program content with that presented here. Again, local users can modify these lists as local curriculum is developed.

Finally, the section entitled "student activities" includes a selection of activities suitable for each instructional topic. This section serves as a starting point for the development of local activities. For further activity ideas, turn to the instructional methods section of this guide. The lists of activities do not include common activities, such as discussion, problem solving, homework (including reading or writing assignments), or small group work, which are suitable student activities for many—if not all—of the instructional topics presented here.

It should be reiterated that these topics are presented as a guide to local curriculum development; local faculty are encouraged to adapt these topics, objectives, contents, and activities to their own instructional needs.

Local Curriculum Development

The following steps will aid local planners in using this section:

1. Become familiar with the identified program goals (see page 28). These goals, which reflect the view of professional traffic safety organizations, are common to all high school driver education programs. The topics, objectives, and content presented in this guide will support those program goals.

2. Determine how your local curriculum is to be structured. Local curriculum should develop around the program goals. Many programs

structure their curriculum into sections or units based on topics such as those presented here.

3. Review the topics, objectives, and content. Identify where in the curriculum those topics will be presented. If sections or units are to be used, determine which topics will be included in each unit or section. The topics presented here can be reorganized to better meet local needs.

4. Determine which topics will be taught in local program phases. Comparison with the topics presented here will help planners determine which to include in the local curriculum. Local instructors are best able to determine which topics and content are most appropriate for their program. Consider local factors that will influence which topics should be addressed in the local program.

5. Refine objectives and select content as needed to ensure that the instruction provided will allow students to achieve objectives determined by local curriculum planners. This, in turn, should help the program achieve overall program goals.

6. Determine time allotments for topics or units, given program time constraints.

7. Conduct periodic assessments of student learning and instruction. Modify objectives, topics, content, activities, and instructional strategies when necessary to ensure optimum student learning.

Introduction to Driver and Traffic Safety Education

To some students, driver education is just another class, but to most, it's the beginning of an experience they have long anticipated. At the same time, the instructor realizes that students are beginning a program of study in a life long skill that will have a profound impact on their lives. The introduction can set the tone for the entire driver and traffic safety education experience. The instructor should strive to communicate to the students how vital the course will be to their future health and to their success as a user of the transportation system.

Objectives	The student should be able to • identify major goals and format of the driver education program • summarize general content and layout of assigned textbooks • explain responsibilities and expectations of driving or observing
Content	• mission and goals of driver and traffic safety education • course policies and procedures, general course organization • overview of the textbook • attendance expectations • on-street instruction procedures — pick up and drop off locations — policies for use of vehicles — appropriate attire — verification of fee payment — issue of student data record card, student driving guide — verification of instruction permit
Student Activities	• Verify information on permit. • Check family vehicle policy. • Complete student data record card. • Develop an introduction sheet for the driver education program. • Develop a textbook contents worksheet.

Introduction to the Highway Transportation System

It is important that students develop a basic understanding of the HTS, its mission, and the functions of the various components of the system. Such an understanding will help students develop an appreciation for their future role in that system. In addition, students should understand that driver education can provide them with the tools, if properly applied, to become safe and responsible members of the HTS.

Objectives	The student should be able to • identify the definition, purpose, and components of the HTS • define a system, explain how the HTS operates as a system • know the "four Es" of the HTS: engineering, enforcement, education, emergency medical services

	• identify the types of roadways that make up the HTS • identify systems related to highway and traffic safety • identify improvements to the HTS • define a break down as it applies to the HTS, describe safety concerns within the HTS
Content	• definition of a system—group of elements forming a complex whole • transportation systems—HTS, water, rail, pipeline, air • meaning of the acronym HTS—highway transportation system and identification of its parts (people, vehicles, roadways) • engineering components — vehicles — roadways and roadsides — traffic management — signs, signals, and markings • enforcement components — speed — alcohol and other drugs — occupant restraints • education components — driver education — driver improvement, enrichment, alcohol and other drug abuse, point reduction classes — public information and education • emergency medical services components • legal system (legislative, judicial) • break downs in the system — traffic jams — crashes and collisions as opposed to accidents — traffic control malfunction • improvements and advancements to systems over the years — operating while intoxicated (OWI) legislation and penalties — occupant restraint laws — minimum drinking age laws — traffic safety enforcement, identification, detection — roadway engineering advancements—highway design features; signs, lighting, and locations; markings; shoulders, medians, off-roadway rumble strips; intelligent vehicle and highway systems — vehicle engineering advancements—front impact bumpers; anti-lock, anti-skid braking systems; supplemental restraint systems; all-wheel traction control; computerization • public information and education—organizations (for example, SADD, MADD), public service announcements, posters and billboards
Student Activities	• Invite guest speakers (for example, law enforcement, engineers). • Students attend a traffic court session and report back to class. • Write research reports.

Licensing Issues

All states have a driver licensing system in place. Though there are a variety of motor vehicle driver's licenses, driver education students need to be most aware of those that apply directly to them and of the requirements that must be met to obtain their license. In most states, students must first obtain an instruction permit. They need to know about the forms, personal documents, and fees necessary for the licensing process.

Driver education instructors must keep in mind that it is the first time the students (and very possibly their parent or guardian) are experiencing the driver licensing process. The licensing process can be confusing to the novice driver and parent or legal guardian. Instructors should strive to provide clear and simple directions for students and their parents or guardians.

Objectives	The student should be able to • identify requirements for instruction permit eligibility • describe the difference between a probationary license and a regular driver's license • identify different types of licenses available • describe the steps required to obtain a probationary license for those under the age of 18 • explain how the Wisconsin point system works and how it applies to those with a probationary license • describe driving restrictions for those with an instruction permit • obtain an instruction permit • list the steps in obtaining a probationary license
Content	• obtaining an instruction permit — required forms, personal documents, and signatures — restrictions • eligibility requirements — age — driver education enrollment — parent or legal guardian signature on notarized Motor Vehicle Department 3001 form • Wisconsin licenses and licensing procedures • Wisconsin point system
Student Activities	• Students take instruction permit test.

Wisconsin Motorist's Handbook and the Law

One component of the state driver's test is the knowledge test, which covers basic traffic laws and rules of Wisconsin. Although the *Wisconsin Motorist's Handbook* presents the basics of the most important rules of the road, instructors need to emphasize that the handbook is not a collection of motor vehicle laws. The actual laws that govern the operation of motor vehicles or driver licensing laws can be found in the Wisconsin Motor Vehicle Codes.

The handbook is available at any vehicle driver licensing testing station, or by contacting the WDOT's distribution center. Refer to the resources list in appendix C.

Objectives	The student should be able to • explain legal speed limits for different types of roadways • describe significance of the shape, symbol, and color of highway signs, signals, markings • summarize basic rules of the road, including right-of-way rules, lane selection, lane positioning for turns, parking requirements • explain alcohol concentration and laws governing the operation of a vehicle while under the influence of alcohol • determine a safe following distance • describe driver blind spots
Content	• instruction permit requirements — age — driver education — forms — personal documents — signatures • Wisconsin rules and laws — signs (meanings of sign shape, color, symbol, location) — markings (color, location) — Wisconsin point system — speed limits — turns (types, lane selection, communication) — lane use and selection — financial responsibility and insurance — alcohol and other drugs (blood alcohol concentration, legal levels, legislation, underage drinking) — safe and legal speeds and following distances — braking and stopping distance — driving in adverse weather conditions — parking (types and requirements) — turnabouts (types and restrictions) — vision (depth perception, night vision, field of vision) • visual perception — looking ahead, to sides, behind — intersection checks — roadside areas — railroad crossings

	— blind spot checks
	— backing
	— window and mirror visibility
	— night vision
	• communication devices
	— lights
	— horn
	— body gestures
	— vehicle positioning
	• adjusting speed to conditions
	• safe space cushions and sharing space
Student Activities	• Study *Wisconsin Motorist's Handbook*. • Take practice test.

Natural Laws

Motor vehicle control depends on several factors. Understanding how natural laws affect one's ability to control a vehicle's direction and stopping distance is vital for safe vehicle operation.

This area of instruction deals with natural laws such as gravity, friction and traction, force of impact, and how speed, tire, and road conditions affect total stopping distances. The ability to control a vehicle depends on more than how quickly a driver responds to a given situation; drivers need to understand how natural laws constantly affect the movements and control of a vehicle.

Objectives	The student should be able to • explain how natural laws (for example, gravity, momentum, kinetic energy, inertia, friction) affect one's ability to control a vehicle • estimate differences in stopping distances for vehicles traveling at different speeds • understand forces that affect a vehicle in a curve and how to safely negotiate a curve • identify ways in which drivers are forewarned of different curves in rural areas • illustrate what is meant by the center of gravity and how this affects a vehicle in a turn • identify steps to test traction • identify vehicle and roadway conditions that affect traction • compare performance capabilities of different types and sizes of vehicles • identify components of total stopping distance • list factors influencing perception and reaction distance • describe factors that determine force of impact • list safety features designed to reduce the force of impact in collisions
Content	• gravity and vehicle control • center of gravity and maneuverability • vehicle capabilities

	• kinetic energy • relationship between speed, stopping distance, and force of impact • road design influence on vehicle control • friction, traction, and vehicle control • tire design, inflation, and tread • road surface and traction • vehicle condition, brakes, steering • vehicle control in curves • perception distance, reaction distance, total stopping distance • natural law effects on stopping distance • estimating total stopping distances under various conditions • components determining force of impact • reducing the force of impact
Student Activities	• Demonstrate vehicle control in a curve. • Demonstrate total stopping distance. • Demonstrate friction and traction.

The Driving Task

Driving and controlling a motor vehicle is not a simple task; the interaction of humans, vehicles, and the driving environment makes driving complex. Students also need to understand that driving is not merely an individual task but also a social task. Safety on the roads for drivers, passengers, and other highway users requires interaction, respect for other motorists, and communication.

Objectives	The student should be able to • explain why the driving task is a mental and social task as well as a physical task • identify requirements to safely operate and control a motor vehicle • identify major mental tasks of driving • explain why driving is a complex task • explain skills and knowledge required for identification, perception, and communication in driving • explain how social, personal, and attitudinal skills are related to driving • define the IPDE (identify, predict, decide, and execute) process • scan and assess traffic situations • perform the IPDE process while tracking and positioning the vehicle • recognize factors that impair the IPDE process • describe elements that contribute to effective visual search techniques • describe classifications of traffic information important to drivers • describe tasks drivers need to master in order to ensure safe operation of a vehicle • define traffic clues and how and where to look for them • describe driver inputs of vehicle control • discuss problems associated with identification of types, locations, and closing potentials of certain vehicles and how to avoid conflict with such vehicles

	• explain how experienced drivers discriminate among sensory stimuli • describe the role experience plays in accurately predicting traffic outcomes • identify elements about which predictions must be made • list courses of action available to drivers • list means of communication with other roadway users • explain techniques for maintaining space and visibility
Content	• essential skills (IPDE) — identify important information in the driving environment while ignoring extraneous sensory stimuli — predict possible and probable actions of other roadway users and consequences of one's own actions — decide on action — execute action and communicate it to others • stored knowledge and perceptual discrimination • social skills development • attitudes • mental aspects of the driving task • identification and interpretation as the guide for action • Smith System — aim high in steering — keep your eyes moving — get the big picture — leave an out — make sure others see you • prediction — actions of other HTS users — response and limitations of driver's vehicle — probable outcomes of action • choices of action, including change in speed or direction, communication, or no change • communication using lights, horn, vehicle position, eye contact, gestures • maintaining space cushion and visibility • fatigue, distraction, impairment, confusion and their effects on the IPDE process
Student Activities	• Quiz on gathering and using information while driving. Students explain each step. • Ask students to provide verbal feedback while driving (commentary driving) emphasizing IPDE.

Visual Checks and Skills

It has been said that 90 percent of driver actions are based on what drivers see. Developing effective visual search and scan skills should be a major objective in all driver education programs. In order to achieve this objective, students must receive instruction and opportunities for practice.

The classroom and simulation phases provide opportunities for such skill development. In addition to being instructed in visual searching and scanning, it is important that students be given opportunities to demonstrate these skills in low risk environments prior to driving. Through the use of discussions, slides, films, and videos, students can be trained and offered opportunities to demonstrate search and scan abilities.

Objectives	The student should be able to • define and describe the IPDE process • identify the Smith System for safe driving • identify roadway conditions, traffic controls, and other highway users that necessitate a change in speed or road position • describe components of an effective visual search pattern • list clues for effective scanning • demonstrate the ten to 15 second scanning rule • demonstrate proper use of mirrors and head checks in establishing and maintaining space cushion • explain the blind spot and conduct blind spot checks • demonstrate safe following distance using following distance rules • list conditions when visibility is reduced • explain strategies to compensate for limited visibility • identify visual abilities needed for safe driving • demonstrate accurate time and space judgments
Content	• defensive driving strategies, including selective seeing • IPDE • visual search pattern • Smith System for safe driving • rear-view mirror and blind spot checks • visual abilities needed for safe driving, including visual acuity, field of vision, depth perception, night vision, color vision, glare, glare recovery • entering traffic gaps and blending smoothly • maintaining a safe space cushion • looking through the curve or turn • scanning and driving in various traffic and roadway conditions • clues (for example, brake lights, back-up lights, signals, traffic signs and lights, eye contact) • types of traffic control devices • interacting with emergency vehicles, joggers, entering and leaving vehicle • intersection right-of-way • quick glance techniques
Student Activities	• Practice visual checks. • Discuss how speed or emotional disturbances may influence scanning ability. • "Freeze" or pause a film in critical situations and ask students to identify and predict potential hazards.

Safety Zones

In order to avoid collision, a driver must be able to stop without colliding with an object, vehicle, or person, or be able to re-direct the vehicle to avoid such an impact. The areas within which these actions can safely be executed are known as safety zones. Safe drivers are always aware of safety zones and traffic and objects around their vehicles or that might intersect their vehicle's path of travel. Maintenance of safety zones around the vehicle is a skill that needs to be taught and reinforced on an ongoing basis.

Objectives	The student should be able to • identify clues to conditions that exist beyond the search pattern and adjust speed and position accordingly • predict what problems might arise • decide not only which vehicle has the right-of-way, but how to safely proceed • execute the appropriate driving decisions • maintain strategies for adequate space cushion while driving in a variety of traffic situations • make appropriate adjustments in speed or position to maintain a space cushion
Content	• vehicle speed adjustment • positioning to reduce hazards • adjustment of vehicle speed and position to isolate risk • judging time and space • safe following distance procedure • developing and maintaining a safe space cushion
Student Activities	• Explain the correct reaction to various intersection situations. • Demonstrate right-of-way situations.

Driver Attitudes, Behaviors, and Risk Management

Research leaves no doubt that driving behaviors are strongly influenced by students' attitudes. Driver and traffic safety educators should help students understand the relationship between attitude and behavior. It is also essential that students gain an understanding of risk and how to make decisions based on potential risk. In order to effectively manage risk, students need to be able to determine and weigh the potential benefits and disadvantages for any given course of action. It is important that students understand that any decision they make—even the decision to refrain from action—involves some risk, and in order to make intelligent and responsible decisions, it is necessary to assess that risk.

Objectives	The student should be able to • define risk and risk management • assess the risk related to different courses of action • identify physical effects of different emotions on drivers, and explain how strong emotions adversely affect a driver's ability to operate a motor vehicle • explain how attitudes affect emotions and behaviors • explain how the IPDE process, properly applied, can reduce risk • identify specific actions that reduce or minimize the likelihood of a crash or sustaining serious injuries or death in the event of a crash
Content	• links between attitudes, emotions, and risks • factors that influence attitudes—knowledge, experience, stage of maturity • definition of risk and risk management • risk assessment: perceived risk versus perceived or potential gain • steps of risk management • behavior selection • behaviors to reduce risk in driving • keeping oneself and one's vehicle fit to drive
Student Activities	• Students take two lists of hypothetical driving situations home. After rating the situations as high, medium, or low risk, students ask a parent or other older driver to rate the second list. Ask students to compare the results, and if some adults gave different ratings than the student, have students discuss the significance of those differences.

Emotions and Self-Control

Strong emotions have a tendency to reduce an individual's ability to respond to situations. Human behavior is influenced by emotions. Because one driver's actions often affects other drivers, pedestrians, and transportation users, the driver has a responsibility to control his or her emotions and behaviors when driving. Students need to learn how strong emotions affect driving behavior so they can reduce the likelihood that anger or other emotions might hinder their ability to safely operate a motor vehicle.

Objectives	The student should be able to • identify the adverse effects of strong emotions on the driving task and on the IPDE process • understand how strong emotions adversely affect an individual's ability to make appropriate decisions and execute actions • describe ways drivers can attempt to deal with emotions so they don't adversely affect their ability to safely control a vehicle • explain the responsibilities passengers have for helping drivers maintain control
Content	• effects of emotions on thinking, reasoning, and judgment • effects of emotions on the IPDE process — identification skills are adversely affected because attention can be fixed, and eye movement decreases — prediction skills are adversely affected as the driver's objectivity and judgment cause emotions to be directed toward other drivers — decision making skills suffer as a result of the narrow focus of attention and a reduction in the number of options under consideration • physical effects of emotion: increased pulse and breathing, sweating, slowed digestion • increased fatigue with prolonged stress • controlling emotions — anticipate emotional situations and adjust expectations — avoid emotional traffic situations by changing schedule or route of travel — limit driving when unfit, tired, or ill — learning from mistakes—one's own and others' — avoid driving when it is impossible to separate emotions from the driving task • practice good driving behavior until it becomes habitual
Student Activities	• Ask students to do the following writing activity: Think of two or more drivers whose driving you have been able to observe over time. Describe the part you think emotions may play in their driving. Consider questions such as: Does the driver belittle the skills or intelligence of other drivers? Does the person blame others for "close calls," or uncomfortable situations? Does the driver "take the mood along" when they drive? Is the driver often rude, or calm and courteous? Does the driver exhibit patience or impatience? Then, think about what you know of the person in circumstances other than driving. Do they behave the same in other circumstances as they do when driving? Finally, describe what lessons from the examination of the behavior of others you might apply to your own driving.

Alcohol and Other Drugs

Alcohol has often been identified as one of the major contributing factors to motor vehicle crashes. In the late 1970s and early 1980s, alcohol was a factor in an estimated 55 to 65 percent of all motor vehicle crashes. In Wisconsin, according to the WDOT (1995), 16 to 20 year olds comprised 8 percent of the total driving population yet were involved in 24 percent of all crashes. In Wisconsin during 1994, a total of 160 drivers killed had blood alcohol levels of .10 percent or higher—37 percent of these were under the age of 21.

Though the percentage of alcohol-related fatalities has declined over the past few decades, thanks to strong societal censure and punishment, significant problems remain, especially in regard to novice drivers. Driver education teachers should collaborate with alcohol and other drug (AOD) education provided elsewhere in the curriculum and in student programs. In addition, instructors need to avoid mixed messages in materials or instruction and strive to select materials and strategies that support a no-use message. Driver education instructors also need to be cognizant of effective instructional strategies that involve students and empower students to adopt behaviors that reduce and eliminate underage alcohol consumption and underage drunk driving.

Students need to understand how alcohol and other drugs impact their ability to see, interpret, make decisions, and respond to situations in the driving environment. Students should also learn about benefits of preventing AOD-related occurrences.

Objectives	The student should be able to • identify traffic safety problems associated with alcohol and other drugs • describe physical and mental effects of alcohol and other drugs on humans and driving performance • define blood alcohol concentration (BAC) and "per se" level of BAC and identify factors that affect BAC • identify OWI and underage drinking laws and penalties — first and subsequent offenses • understand how mass media and peer pressure influence alcohol consumption • develop refusal skills • identify and apply techniques to reduce peer pressure to drink or use other drugs • identify alternatives to underage drinking and driving while under the influence of AOD • define implied consent, zero tolerance, and Wisconsin's "not-a-drop" law
Content	• alcohol-related motor vehicle crash data • comparisons of OWI, alcohol-related traffic violations across age groups • losses incurred as a result of alcohol-related crashes • physical and emotional effects of AOD — blood system (pressure, bleeding/clotting) — central nervous system — body organs (liver, heart, brain, and so forth) — IPDE process — perception — loss of inhibitions • legal intoxication • BAC and intoxication • impairment versus intoxication

- zero tolerance
- factors affecting BAC
  — body size and weight
  — emotions
  — personal health
  — food
  — strength of drinks
  — time elapsed
  — elimination rates and time
  — presence of other drugs
  — tolerance
- OWI laws and penalties
  — first, second, third offenses, and habitual violator
  — fines
  — driving privilege suspension or revocation
- underage laws and penalties for AOD use
- effect of peer pressure on behavior
  — others' influence on decision making
  — resisting peer pressure, alternative activities
- media influence on behavior

Student Activities

- Demonstrate and assess reaction distance and total stopping distance in a variety of conditions and situations, including alcohol impairment.
- Role play and practice refusal skill strategies and dealing with peer pressure.

Physical Conditions of Drivers

In order to obtain and maintain a driver's license, drivers must be physically able to operate a motor vehicle in traffic. Occasionally, drivers are subject to physical (or mental) conditions that affect their driving ability. Instruction about physical conditions of drivers should emphasize the physical demands and requirements of driving. Students can learn about how physically-challenged drivers make use of driver control technologies and about the resources available for those in need of special services or devices.

Objectives	The student should be able to • identify various health-related conditions that affect one's ability to drive • identify physical abilities that are required for driving and the importance of periodic physical examinations • identify physical handicaps and the adaptive equipment that allows those with handicaps to drive • describe state requirements and medical review procedures following an incident that may impair one's ability to safely operate a vehicle • identify examples of illness or injury and how the driving task may be affected • identify physical conditions that impair vision
Content	• conditions—fatigue, illness • carbon monoxide • aging • vision—visual acuity, field of vision, color vision, depth perception, night vision • impaired hearing • physical limitations, effects on driving
Student Activities	• Use vision charts to check vision. • Use wheelchairs to see and feel what it is like to be physically impaired. • Discuss symptoms of chronic illness and aging and effects on driving ability.

Occupant Restraint Systems

Annually, more people are killed and injured due to motor vehicle crashes than for any other single cause. A significant number of deaths and serious injuries could be avoided if drivers and passengers always used occupant restraints. Although significant progress has been made in increasing the percentage of people who use occupant restraints, there is still room for improvement. Driver and traffic safety education programs have played—and will continue to play—a key role in encouraging drivers to always use occupant restraints. In addition, driver and traffic safety education emphasizes the responsibilities drivers have in ensuring that all passengers use occupant restraints.

Objectives	The student should be able to • identify the different types of occupant restraints and systems • describe the laws governing occupant restraints and those responsible for ensuring that all passengers are properly restrained • discuss the benefits of occupant restraints and how they not only protect passengers and drivers, but also help the driver maintain vehicle control • describe the difference between primary and secondary enforcement of occupant restraint laws • describe how safety belts and airbags are activated in the event of a crash • define passive and active restraint systems • list occupant restraints for adults or children • list procedures for adjusting restraint systems for safety and comfort • list and refute safety belt myths • explain first and second collisions
Content	• occupant restraints—safety belt, shoulder belt, lap belt, head restraint, automatic safety belt, shoulder belt attached to door or to track, shoulder and lap belt attached to door, airbag, infant and child safety seat • classification of occupant restraints — passive restraints — active restraints • adult and child restraint laws • primary and secondary enforcement • first and second collisions
Student Activities	• Demonstrate a child safety seat. • "Convincer" or "roll-over demonstrator."

Signs, Signals, and Markings

Traffic controls come in many different types, shapes, styles, and colors. They are important components in the HTS as they inform, regulate, and warn drivers of requirements, situations, and services. Without traffic controls, safe, efficient travel would be much more

Objectives	difficult. Knowing the locations and meanings of traffic controls increases the safety and ease with which the transportation system is used. The student should be able to • explain the meanings of highway signs or signals by their shape, color, and symbol • identify location of certain signs along roadways • classify signs as regulatory, warning, or guide • explain methods of signal operation • understand legal meaning and sequence of signal lights • explain the differences between traffic intersections that are timed or weight activated • define a controlled or protected turn signal • define legal stop position • diagram pavement markings and understand their purposes • design a speed chart for highway settings
Content	• signs—colors, shapes, symbols, classifications (regulatory, warning, guide) • speed limits • interpreting signs—highway, exit, and mile marker numbering; directions; distances; types of services; lane use; pedestrian; handicapped • international signs • signal lights/traffic control—progressive or timed, sensored or actuated, pedestrian activated, sequential • legal and practical meanings of signals—solid, flashing, arrows, legal stop position • pavement markings—colors, dashed or solid, other markings, limited access, shared left turn lane, reversible lanes, reflectors/delineators
Student Activities	• Design games or activities. • Prepare flash cards or slides (using color, shape, or symbol) to develop quick response.

Enforcement

Most drivers will—at some stage in their driving careers—find themselves involved in a situation involving law enforcement officers. When such situations occur, drivers will be better prepared for such interaction if they understand the traffic law enforcement process.

Objectives	The student should be able to • explain concepts of basic speed law and minimum and maximum speed limits • understand the purpose of police enforcement and techniques • follow safe and cooperative guidelines for interacting with law enforcement personnel
Content	• police and enforcement • public attitude toward traffic enforcement • purpose of laws and the role of police • procedures to follow when stopped by law enforcement—come to safe stop, stay in vehicle, stay calm, minimize reaching movements/don't hide objects from police, be in control of passenger, be cooperative, leave scene in a safe manner • factors that may affect an officer's decision • types of enforcement—warnings (verbal and written), citations, arrest • speed and alcohol enforcement and devices
Student Activities	• Guest speaker from law enforcement agency.

Intersections and Right-of-Way Laws

According to the Fatal Accident Reporting System of the NHTSA (1990), 23 percent of fatal crashes nationwide occur at intersections, with more than one-third of those occurring at uncontrolled intersections. About 52 percent of rural fatal crashes occur at intersections controlled by stops signs, and nearly 39 percent of urban fatal crashes occur at intersections controlled by signals. In Wisconsin, nearly 28 percent of all fatal crashes occurred at intersections. Intersection collisions accounted for 36 percent of all Wisconsin crashes reported in 1990 (WDOT, 1991).

Driver education classes should emphasize that intersections need to be handled with care. Students need to be taught how to identify and respond to intersections. Students should never assume, for example, that crossing traffic will yield the right-of-way, regardless of existing traffic controls; right-of-way is a behavior that should never be taken for granted.

Objectives	The student should be able to • explain what is meant by right-of-way and how to determine who should be given right-of-way • describe problems encountered with motorcyclists regarding right-of-way • define controlled and uncontrolled intersections • explain or demonstrate correct lane positions for turning and proceeding through intersections using diagrams of intersections and traffic markings

	• discuss or demonstrate safe visual search patterns for approaching different types of intersections • understand the amount of time it takes to complete a left or right turn, or proceed straight through an intersection, and why it is important to select an appropriate gap in traffic before proceeding into an intersection • describe stopping locations at intersections and behind other vehicles at an intersection • identify lane positioning for beginning a turn and proceeding after a turn at a multiple-lane intersection • explain or demonstrate how to approach an intersection and react appropriately to other roadway users • apply right-of-way principles at intersections • determine when it is safe and legal to turn right on red • identify railroad-related signs, signals, and responsibilities at railroad crossings • demonstrate an understanding of the principle of "last clear chance" and how this applies to intersections and right-of-way • position the vehicle in median openings when crossing or leaving divided roadways • identify and respond to roadway characteristics that may create hazards
Content	• lane selection and vehicle positioning in intersections • approaching, entering, and exiting from uncontrolled intersections, as well as intersections controlled with stop signs, signal lights, yield signs, pavement markings • determining right-of-way • choosing a gap in crossing or joining traffic • stopping location for control signs • visual search patterns at intersections • right and left turns to and from multiple-lane streets • right-of-way principles and situations • obeying traffic signs, signals, and devices at intersections • railroad crossing procedures • "last clear chance" principle • right turn on red • reacting safely to complex intersections • identifying intersection conflicts
Student Activities	• Students develop a series of intersection diagrams and insert possible sign, signals, and markings. Afterwards, students place vehicles in each design and determine rights-of-way. Or students can walk through each situation in the classroom, gym, or cafeteria. • Students list and illustrate intersection designs. • Students define "right-of-way" and the underlying principles and traffic situations to which right-of-way applies. • Drive through various types of intersections. • Show correct positioning in median openings when crossing, entering, or leaving divided highways. • Discuss right-of-way and the fact that right-of-way is not a guarantee.

Vehicle and Instrument Orientation

Drivers should be familiar with the vehicle they drive. Each vehicle is composed of a number of systems for control, comfort, safety, and communications. Each system has its own specific purpose; knowing the location and purpose of the instruments and controls, and being able to operate those controls without looking away from the road increases driver safety and comfort.

Objectives	The student should be able to • demonstrate proper vehicle approach • describe the procedures for performing a visual vehicle safety inspection • locate, identify, and utilize instruments and vehicle controls • locate a control without looking, while seated behind the wheel of the family vehicle • explain the major classifications of vehicle controls (safety, comfort, communication) and classify the controls • identify and explain the warning lights and gauges found on the instrument panel • describe devices that enhance comfort in your vehicle • describe use of the gear selector and gears • list vehicle components that aid visibility • explain checks to make before and after entering a vehicle • explain the use of all gears
Content	• approach to the vehicle • vehicle control checklist • informational controls—instrument panel, alternator warning light or gauge, brake system warning light, fuel gauge, high beam indicator light, odometer (including trip odometer), oil pressure warning light or gauge, safety belt warning light, speedometer (digital, heads-up, gauge), temperature light or gauge, turn signal indicators, tachometer • operational controls—instrument panel, ignition and starter switch, steering wheel (tilt, telescopic), selector lever (automatic transmission), gear shift lever (manual transmission), parking brake and release, clutch pedal, brake pedal, accelerator pedal, cruise control, emergency flashers control • other safety devices—door locks and windows (manual and electric), window lock out, windshield washers and wipers, traction control devices, fog lights, headlights (halogen and standard), defroster • communication devices—parking lights, running lights, turn signal lever and lane change indicator, horn • comfort devices—sun visor, seat adjustment, heater, air conditioning, and audio controls • other devices and controls—dimmer switch, overhead light switch, hood release lever, gas tank cover release lever, trunk release, map light
Student Activities	• Written checklist for family vehicle. • Drawing of dashboard and controls.

Pre-Start

Before starting a vehicle, it is important that the driver conduct proper pre-start procedures. These include closing and locking the doors, adjusting the seat and mirrors, and fastening restraint devices. In addition, drivers should take the responsibility of ensuring that all passengers secure themselves by fastening their restraint devices. Students should be warned that airbags alone are not adequate protection.

Objectives	The student should be able to • display an instruction permit prior to driving • conduct a visual safety check in the area of the vehicle • enter the vehicle safely • perform pre-start procedures
Content	• display of instruction permits • safety check—area surrounding vehicle, vehicular physical damage, tire pressure, fluid leaks/stains, entering the vehicle in a safe manner, pre-start procedures and checklist, key in switch, lock doors, seat and mirror adjustment, use of occupant restraint devices, head restraint (if applicable), parking brake
Student Activities	• Demonstrate pre-start safety check. • Design a pre-start checklist. • Students present instruction permits.

Starting Engine

Starting the engine is an important step. Teaching the students how to quickly check important instruments or gauges is also an important component to cover before a vehicle is put in motion. Students should also know whether the vehicle's choke is automatic or manual. Drivers should be reminded to consult the owner's manual regarding warm-up or idling time before moving the vehicle. Today, many manufacturers suggest slow driving as the best way to warm-up the engine; for these vehicles, idling only wastes fuel and causes unnecessary pollution.

Objectives	The student should be able to • start the vehicle, using appropriate steps • demonstrate ability to determine that an engine is running
Content	• ignition switch location and use • accelerator • brake, parking brake • battery

Putting Vehicle in Motion, Steering

Before putting a vehicle in motion, drivers need to make sure that their path is free of obstacles or vehicular traffic. Instruction in communicating intentions, checking traffic, and moving into the flow of traffic need to be emphasized and reinforced throughout the classroom and laboratory phases of instruction, until such practices become habitual.

Objectives	The student should be able to • demonstrate procedures for putting a vehicle in motion • demonstrate effective steering techniques • safely back the vehicle along a straight line
Content	• vehicle starting procedure • putting the vehicle in motion • steering—hand-over-hand • stopping • backing in a straight line
Student Activities	• Observation of other drivers.

Turns

Directing a vehicle in a straight line is one thing, learning how to turn and maintain control of a vehicle is another. Instruction about turns needs to include discussion of communication and vehicle positioning prior to, during, and while completing a turn. Novice drivers need to be aware of hazards of both right and left turns.

Objectives	The student should be able to • demonstrate hand-over-hand method of steering • make right and left turns at intersections • check traffic on cross streets • time turns through gaps in traffic • understand the use of four-lane and left turn bays or "storage lanes" • demonstrate speed control • execute a lane change
Content	• hand-over-hand steering • scanning and reacting safely to intersections • right and left turn procedures • visual search pattern using "left, right, left, go" • positioning for right and left turns • blending smoothly and safely • right and left turns using cones, uncontrolled intersections, through street, yield sign, stop sign
Student Activities	• Hand-over-hand steering drill. • Demonstrate lane positioning and left and right turns. • Demonstrate using cones in a forward serpentine.

Advanced Backing and Turnabouts

Backing a car can be a difficult procedure for novice drivers. Instructors need to help create an awareness of the challenge. In some vehicles, drivers have difficulty determining where the bumper of the vehicle is located. Thus it is not unusual for drivers to collide with another vehicle or object while backing.

A turnabout is an exercise which can be used to turn a vehicle around instead of having to go around a block. Though going around the block may be safer, in some instances it is not possible or practical. Teaching students how to determine which turnabout is safest for any given situation will prove valuable in their future driving experiences.

Objectives	The student should be able to • execute serpentine course • demonstrate procedures for backing to the left and right • explain and demonstrate the proper procedures for completing a Y-turn (three-point turnabout) • demonstrate additional turnabouts as optional activities—backing into driveway or alley, going around the block • execute visual checks when backing
Content	• backing while turning left or right • using focal point • backing into driveways or alley • two-point turnabout • figure eight both forward and backward • T-exercise procedures • turnabout or Y-turn (three-point turnabout) • X-exercise
Student Activities	• Back through serpentine course. • Back left and right with only slight steering. • Demonstrate Y-turn and other optional turnabouts. • Observation of other drivers.

Parking

Parking is an activity conducted every time a driver completes a trip and prepares to secure a vehicle. There are several different types of parking exercises, and as many as possible should be presented to novice drivers. Most parking requires skilled actions in limited spaces, thus additional practice outside of class will be valuable in developing students' parking skills.

Objectives	The student should be able to • perform the steps required to enter, navigate, and exit a parking structure • demonstrate procedures for entering and exiting angle and parallel parking spaces • secure the vehicle after parking • stop and start smoothly on a hill without rollback • demonstrate procedures for parking uphill and downhill—with and without curb • re-enter traffic from the parked position
Content	• parking—angle, perpendicular, parallel, backing, or pulling into a parking space • enter, navigate, and exit parking structure • lane position on approach • depth perception to the front, sides, and rear • rear-wheel tracking • seating position while backing and maneuvering in reverse • securing vehicle • parking uphill and downhill, with and without a curb • hill stop and start • re-entering traffic from the parked position • parking brake
Student Activities	• Demonstrate parking—angle, perpendicular, parallel, backing into space, pulling into space. • Garage exercise.

Securing and Leaving the Vehicle

Securing and leaving the vehicle—though one of the easier tasks to perform—is important for vehicle and personal safety. Any time a vehicle is parked, drivers need to be aware of security factors of the vehicle and themselves. Parking in well lit areas reduces the potential for vehicle theft and vandalism. Also, the closer drivers can park to their destination, the less time they will be exposed to potential dangers of the street.

Objectives	The student should be able to • demonstrate correct procedures for parking and leaving a vehicle
Content	• securing the vehicle • exiting the vehicle

Sharing the Roadway with Others

Consider the variety of vehicles that travel the streets, roads, and highways. Drivers have to share the roadway with vehicles of all types, from two-wheeled bicycles to 18-wheelers. Each vehicle that uses the roadway has different characteristics, and drivers who are aware of the limitations of various vehicles can use the information to add an extra margin of safety for all concerned.

Motorcycles and bicycles, for example, present their own special considerations. It is important to know that these vehicles are difficult to see, especially at night, and that cycle operators have very little personal protection. Automobile and truck drivers need to consider these factors and use search and scan techniques to identify cyclists and leave ample safety zones between themselves and cyclists. Drivers also need to appreciate the restricted vision of most tractor-trailer operators due to the size of their trailers. Vehicles following too closely behind or alongside such a vehicle, especially during a rain, may be difficult to see. This, in turn, could cause a problem should the tractor-trailer operator need to brake or make a sudden lane change. These examples illustrate that being aware of other vehicles' capabilities and limitations can help drivers operate safely when they share the roads with those vehicles.

Objectives The student should be able to
- list different types of roadway users and strategies to consider when interacting with each
- demonstrate to other drivers acts of courtesy that avoid conflicts
- explain control limitations of different vehicles and make decisions that take those limitations into account
- avoid dangerous conflicts by positioning one's vehicle to assist other drivers
- identify and describe blind spots of various vehicles and demonstrate ability to avoid driving in others' blind spots
- recognize when the front, sides, and rear zones are open, closed, or in transition
- describe how motorcycles and cars differ in handling ability and maneuverability
- describe clues for identifying the presence of two-wheeled vehicles
- explain how riders of two-wheeled vehicles can reduce conflicts with other roadway users
- list the protective equipment necessary for a motorcycle or moped user
- describe clues for identifying the presence of pedestrians
- list the dangers of interacting with large trucks
- identify various hazards posed by overtaking tractor-trailers
- explain procedures to follow when approaching or being approached by an emergency vehicle
- describe how to follow and pass large trucks
- explain how to treat a school bus with flashing lights
- discuss potential of encountering snowmobiles or all-terrain vehicles in rural areas
- demonstrate use of outside mirrors
- demonstrate safe lane change procedures

Content
- developing accurate mirror-reading skills to overcome blind spot problems
- understanding and compensating for mirror distortions

	• safe passing, lane changing, merging, backing, and blending smoothly in a variety of traffic environments with a van, truck, or other large vehicle • early identification and prediction skills and techniques • projection of imaginary safety zones around the vehicle • maintaining adequate space (zone control) and reacting when trapped by inadequate space • small cars • buses • mass transit and school buses—laws, passengers entering and exiting, bus stops • motorcycles, mopeds and scooters, and bicycles—visibility, where to look for motorcycles, size and weight differences, maneuverability, speed, stopping distance, handling traits, lane position, following distance, passing, roadway surfaces, adverse weather, crossing railroad tracks, carrying passengers, rider apparel and protective equipment, laws • pedestrians—children, senior citizens, joggers, rights at crosswalks and intersections, walking, bus stops, parking lot, school zones • delivery vehicles, vans, pick up trucks, other trucks, recreational vehicles—size, weight, visibility, following distance, laws, passing, meeting, maneuverability, stopping distance • snowmobiles and all-terrain vehicles—crossing highways, speed, protective apparel, laws • animals—where to look and what to look for, time of day, dangers of large and small animals, avoiding collisions, how to collide when unavoidable • emergency vehicles—approaching or being approached by an emergency vehicle
Student Activities	• Demonstrate space cushion maintenance. • Review common collision situations in which failure to control space was the key problem. • Walk a designated route and write a summary report of experiences as a pedestrian. • "Freeze" or pause a film in critical situations and ask students to identify visibility problems. • Demonstrate blind spots.

Lane Changes

Changing lanes is one of the most common high risk maneuvers drivers perform on a regular basis. Driver educators need to provide students with experience in changing lanes so that proper search and scan, acceleration, and communication techniques become habitual.

Objectives	The student should be able to • determine appropriate lane selection • perform right and left lane changes • demonstrate steering for lane changes • perform mirror usage and signaling for lane changes • demonstrate blind spot checks
Content	• lane selection • lane change procedures • effects of steering, signaling, visual search patterns, mirror usage, blind spot checks, following distance on lane changing

Passing

Passing another vehicle on a two-lane, two-way roadway is one of the most hazardous and dangerous maneuvers for drivers—especially novice drivers. Unfortunately, it is difficult to provide students with passing experience during driver education. Often, driver education vehicles are passed by other drivers, but only rarely does the novice driver get to practice this skill. Whenever possible, passing should be taught and students should have experience with passing, even if it is simulated or controlled using two driver education vehicles. The essential skills required deal with open spaces, communicating intentions, acceleration, and steering. In every situation, students should be able to evaluate the legality, safety, and value of passing.

Objectives	The student should be able to • conduct a passing maneuver using appropriate procedures • use vehicle communication devices while passing a vehicle and returning to the proper lane • use blind spot and head checks prior to passing and returning to the correct lane
Content	• factors to consider when determining whether or not to pass—safety, legality, value • pre-passing visual checks to front, rear, sides • mirror usage • use of directional signals and horn • blind spot and head checks • acceleration and speed control • steering
Student Activities	• Practice controlled passing on left. • Practice static lane change and overtake (useful in cases of a stalled vehicle in front). • Practice dynamic lane change (passing a moving vehicle).

Communicating with Other Drivers

Safe, courteous, and defensive driving are attributes all driver education programs attempt to develop in novice drivers. One important related driving skill is communication with other drivers.

By law, drivers in Wisconsin are required to signal their intention to turn at least 100 feet before they turn. In the event a vehicle's turn signals are not functioning, drivers are required to use appropriate hand signals. In addition to turn signals, there are several other ways drivers can communicate to each other. Two of those include vehicle positioning and speed. Teaching students the importance of vehicle positioning can greatly enhance their ability to communicate with other vehicle operators. By observing a vehicle's position and speed, drivers are provided information that can help them determine how to respond to or interact with the vehicle.

Objectives	The student should be able to • demonstrate communication devices, including lights, parking lights, brake lights, turn signals, emergency flashers, and horn • explain how vehicle position, eye contact, and body gestures can promote communication between drivers • demonstrate communication skills • identify situations in which risk of collision is increased by a lack of communication • describe ways to confirm that communication has been received and understood
Content	• communication tools • characteristics of effective communication • situations in which communication is vital to safe driving • reducing risk through timely communications • vehicle positioning

Evasive Action

It is likely that drivers will, at some time, face an emergency situation that will require an immediate response in order to avoid a collision with an object, animal, or person in their path of travel.

Consider these situations: A deer suddenly runs out in front of a vehicle traveling on a rural road or interstate. Or a driver decides to pass another vehicle, but fails to identify an approaching vehicle, or misjudges the size of the gap. In such situations, evasive action may be necessary in order to avoid collision. Of course, ideally drivers never have to resort to evasive action, but the odds are that such a need will arise at some time for every driver. Driver education programs need to address evasive actions and the procedures for taking such actions.

Objectives	The student should be able to • identify roadway hazards • demonstrate driving skills necessary for avoiding other roadway users
Content	• roadway hazard identification—objects, potholes, vehicles, animals, people • evasive steering
Student Activities	• Drive on roadways with various hazards (real or simulated). More advanced exercises can involve the addition of simulated traffic.

Driving a Standard Transmission

For most novice drivers, learning to drive a vehicle with standard transmission presents significant challenges. Nonetheless, those who learn how to operate a standard transmission will gain the skills to drive a wider range of vehicles in the future.

Though there is little argument that knowing how to drive a standard transmission vehicle is of great value, very few driver education vehicles are of the standard transmission type. Local programs should consider whether to provide students stick-shift driving instruction. Districts are encouraged to consider ways to provide the opportunity for those who need to learn stick-shift driving—even if it is limited to an off-street area.

Objectives	The student should be able to • demonstrate proper shifting technique and friction point • coordinate the clutch, accelerator, brake, and gear shift lever • demonstrate smooth blending with traffic • identify the speed problems and differences of driving a standard transmission vehicle
Content	• pre-driving and securing procedures • gear patterns • use of clutch, friction point • starting, putting the vehicle in motion, downshifting, stopping • safe backing • blending smoothly with traffic • stopping and starting on a hill • special problems • "riding the clutch"
Student Activities	• Review owner's manual for special driving tips and strategies. • Practice simulated standard transmission shifting.

Adverse Conditions

Many driver education programs do not provide students practice driving in adverse conditions. In part, this may be due to the fact that providing instruction in adverse conditions is difficult. No one can be certain of weather conditions. Driving in adverse weather conditions also increases risk levels of instruction. Driver educators have to walk the fine line of presenting a message of safety while also providing some experiences for students in adverse conditions.

Though weather cannot be controlled, one adverse condition which drivers can experience is darkness. Night driving experience is important; according to the AAA, though young drivers only do about 20 percent of their driving at night, crashes during the night account for nearly 80 percent of all novice driver crashes (AAA, 1996). Of course, many factors can influence whether students will receive instruction in night driving; in districts where students travel long distances by bus to and from school, driving is often limited to regular school hours. Whenever possible, programs should encourage novice drivers to gain a wide range of driving experiences—yet take into account the amount of risk.

Objectives	The student should be able to • adapt visual search patterns to darkness • maintain lane position and speed control • check traffic signs, anticipate environmental changes, and observe traffic • demonstrate the appropriate reaction to traffic hazards • identify driver actions to ensure a safe following distance in adverse conditions • explain effects of different weather conditions on vehicle control • identify specific driver actions to compensate for adverse weather • describe the different types of skids and why they occur • explain procedures to regain control of a vehicle in a skid • explain what is meant by threshold braking, and how to utilize a vehicle's brakes (for vehicles with or without anti-lock brakes) • describe where ice is most likely to appear first on roadways • define black ice • explain corrective actions for various adverse driving conditions (snow, rain, flooding, hail, wind, fog, and so forth) • assess how visibility is affected by different light conditions • explain why darkness is considered an adverse condition • use high and low beams as warranted by traffic; avoid over driving headlights • demonstrate precautions and procedures unique to night driving • adjust vehicle speed to compensate for reduced visibility • use the "identify and predict" strategy in dealing with hazards that are obscured or concealed by darkness • describe strategies and techniques for safe driving in adverse conditions—night, low light, glare, rain, fog, snow, wind, construction areas • explain preparations for seasonal changes
Content	• mirror—night or day setting • headlights—high and low beam, over driving headlights • street light and sign illumination • four second following distance rule • meeting other vehicles

	• use of lights and wipers • limited visibility, night visibility • preparing for seasonal change • preparing for trouble—auto emergency kit • behavior changes resulting from environmental (weather) changes • threshold braking • traction on snow, ice, or under rainy conditions or temperature changes • skid recovery procedures, including all-wheel, front-wheel, and rear-wheel drive vehicles • adverse conditions, including night driving, and the IPDE process • snow—effects of changing temperatures, stuck in snow, snowbound • areas to watch for ice—bridges and overpasses, shade, and intersections • effects of changing temperatures • skidding—types and causes, prevention, reactions • hydroplaning • construction zones—workers, speed limit • other conditions—rain and wet pavement, fog, deep water, "black ice," "summer ice," extreme heat or cold, wind, dawn and dusk
Student Activities	• Observe headlight illumination on high and low beam. • Demonstrate skidding and stopping. • Students present examples of their own experiences with adverse conditions or limited visibility. • Discuss how weather changes invoke behavior changes. • Define over driving headlights, rocking the car, locked wheel, and torque steer. • Discuss adjusting driving habits and skills at night and in other adverse conditions.

Emergency Procedures

Responding quickly and appropriately to an emergency can mean the difference between life and death. Though traffic emergency situations are not common events, they do occur. Consider some of the following situations: a stalled vehicle on a railroad track; an inattentive driver whose vehicle is drifting off the road; a car at a stop being approached by another vehicle coming too fast to stop; a fast-moving vehicle experiencing a front-wheel blowout. In each of these situations, actions taken immediately can reduce the likelihood of a crash or reduce the severity of damage and loss of life.

Though students cannot always be provided with hands-on experiences in dealing with emergencies, instruction can help them prepare for the occasional emergency. Students can learn how to react and respond to different emergencies through instruction and simulated practice. Planning for emergencies should be a part of every driver education program—the knowledge gained could save lives.

Objectives	The student should be able to • identify vehicle emergencies and actions required in those emergencies • explain how to cross railroad tracks legally and safely • discuss what to do when encountering animals along the roadway • describe the correct procedures for using jumper cables • identify actions to take in emergencies such as going off the road, submersion, imminent collision, railroad crossing malfunction, downed high voltage wires, or losing control in a curve • demonstrate reactions to skids, brake failure, steering failure, tire blowout, loss of lights, hood failure, stuck accelerator, flooded engine, stall on railway crossing, overheated engine, fire, windshield failure, off-road recovery • identify proper use of vehicle controls to combat adverse conditions—wipers, lights, tire chains, defroster
Content	• dangers—brake failure, steering failure, loss of lights, hood failure, stuck accelerator, flooded engine, stalled (and stalled on railroad tracks), overheated engine, car fire, off-road recovery, brake failure, dirt on windshield, high voltage, submersion, potholes, animals, pedestrians, deep water across road, tire blowout, human errors, railroad crossing malfunctions • skids (front-, rear-, and all-wheel drive) • controlled brake/swerve (crash avoidance) • collision—head on, side impact, rear end • proper use of vehicle controls—wipers, defroster • tires—chains, changing • dead battery and jumper cable procedures
Student Activities	• Students review traffic crashes in their local paper to analyze which of the crashes involved adverse conditions or equipment failure. • Demonstrate brake failure.

Escape Routes

It is important that drivers learn to "have an out," or maintain an open area in which to direct their vehicle in the event of an obstacle or other emergency. This open area is a "safety zone"; the path the operator takes to move the vehicle into the safety zone is known as an "escape route."

Novice drivers need to gain experience with visual search and scan skills necessary to ensure safe escape routes. Maintaining an awareness of the environment surrounding the vehicle and always keeping at least one area open and accessible are the first steps in establishing an escape route and safety zone.

Objectives	The student should be able to • explain the need to plan ahead and remain alert for safe escapes from dangerous situations • make early identification of potential hazards • quickly locate the escape path of least damaging consequences • execute driving actions to avoid or minimize the effects of collision • identify hazards, predict their effects, and decide how to act • execute defensive driving maneuvers in time to avoid conflict
Content	• identifying safety zones and escape routes • common dangerous situations from which drivers must escape • evasive action maneuvers • need for constant awareness and defensive driving
Student Activities	• Demonstrate escape options. • "Freeze" or pause a film in critical situations and discuss crash avoidance techniques.

Crash Responsibilities

Despite the belief that most traffic crashes are avoidable events, crashes do occur. Though a major goal of operating a motor vehicle is to avoid being involved in a collision, unfortunately, the potential for collision exists whenever a vehicle is placed in motion. Knowing what, or what not, to do or say can be valuable to a driver involved in a collision.

Regardless of who is at fault, individuals involved in a collision need to know and understand their responsibilities. Some simple guidelines and procedures can help those involved stay calm and prevent further threats to their safety and well being and that of others. Novice drivers should understand their responsibilities, from rendering assistance to the injured, securing the crash scene, and sharing required information with others involved in the collision, to completing necessary crash reports with the police and insurance agencies. If drivers know their responsibilities and follow appropriate procedures, they will be better able to protect themselves against legal litigation and personal loss.

Objectives	The student should be able to • identify procedures to follow in reporting a crash in which they are involved • list information to share with other drivers when involved in a crash • describe safety procedures to follow upon discovery of a crash, including safety and protection of victims, and traffic control • describe first aid procedures • describe implications of the "good Samaritan law"
Content	• procedures if involved in a collision—stop in a safe place (out of traffic if possible); turn off ignition; engage emergency flashers, warning triangles, flares; check to see if anyone is injured; determine severity of injuries; give aid and comfort to the injured; avoid moving the injured if possible; have someone call police and medical authorities; call 911 (if available and needed); exchange information with others involved (for example, name, address, phone number, insurance company, agent, policy number, driver's license number, license plate number); get names, addresses, and phone numbers of witnesses; seek medical attention for yourself if needed • procedures upon arriving at the scene of a collision — responsibilities — "good Samaritan law" — ensuring one's own safety — park in a safe place (past crash scene if possible), don't become an additional victim — keep occupants calm and tell them help has been called • check neurological status of victim • ask victim to wiggle toes or fingers • do not ask victim to move head or neck • it is best to avoid moving occupants from vehicle • treat shock—keep victim warm, have them lie down and raise feet for better circulation (if victim does not appear to have other injuries)

	• if first aid is necessary, use the ABC priority system—Airway (must be open and clear), Breathing (look for chest rising and falling, listen for air, feel for air coming out of nose and mouth), Circulation (check pulse, administer CPR if trained) and bleeding control (pressure and elevation). Note: Unless it is a life or death situation, avoid exposure to bodily fluids—use gloves or other buffering material when applying pressure to an open wound.
Student Activities	• Discuss legal responsibilities and the "good Samaritan law." • Interview or invite an emergency medical technician as a guest speaker. Ask what injuries are most common, what kinds of first aid treatments are most frequently administered, and what new techniques are used for lifesaving. • Ask a Red Cross instructor to be a guest speaker.

Rural Roadways

Although rural, city, and limited access roadways have much in common, they also have significant differences. For that reason, these roadway categories are separately addressed here. Instructors can take advantage of these categories to explain, and to have students explore, the similarities and differences of driving in these different environments.

A significant portion of the HTS is comprised of rural roadways. Driving along rural roads, consisting mainly of narrow two-lane roads, presents numerous challenges. Understanding the numerous challenges and limitations drivers are confronted with on rural roadways and in rural environments can help drivers adapt to rural driving.

State legislation requires that driver education programs in Wisconsin provide instruction in the hazards posed by farm equipment and animals on highways. Therefore, instructors need to ensure that their programs include instruction on these hazards. It is important that students learn about the handling characteristics and limitations of large equipment so that drivers can make informed decisions about how to respond to large farm vehicles and other equipment.

Students also need to be prepared to encounter animals on or near the road. Collisions with animals—especially deer—are quite common. Students should know how to minimize the likelihood of animal–vehicle collisions and how to deal with losses resulting from such collisions.

Objectives	The student should be able to • describe rural highway characteristics that create problems for the unfamiliar driver • explain why the rural environment has twice the fatality rate as city traffic • discuss hazards posed by farm equipment and animals • identify basic skills and highway design features relevant to rural driving • identify highway users that present special problems for the rural driver and problems associated with each • identify rural roadway hazards
Content	• speeds for rural or country driving • rural roadway types and surfaces

	• encountering rural hazards such as railroad crossings, hills, school buses, cyclists, tailgaters, construction zones, animals, and slow-moving vehicles • visual search pattern for country roads • special characteristics of two-lane roads • curves, hills, and limited sight distances • passing–no passing zones, deciding and preparing to pass (two-lane roads and multiple-lane roads), judging oncoming traffic, safe passing and being passed, passing maneuvers • hazards of driving at night on rural roads • rural railroad crossings • driving in the mountains and desert • federal, state, and county highways; town and gravel roads
Student Activities	• Develop a rural driving strategies worksheet. • Students view photographs, slides, or video tape of rural scenes and identify potential hazards. • Discuss differences in traffic signs, signals, and markings on rural roads. • Students apply the IPDE process to rural driving. • Select one or two students to make a chart depicting the steps for passing on two-lane roads and multiple-lane rural roads. • List the hazards of driving on rural roads at night or in adverse weather conditions. • Divide the class into two groups and have them present the differences between mountain and desert driving. • Demonstrate negotiation of a high speed curve. • Demonstrate passing procedures.

City Driving and Traffic

Anyone who has ever driven in a large city or urban area can identify factors that make driving in such environments a challenge. Regardless of where people live, it is likely they will have a need, at some time in their driving careers, to drive in a congested urban environment. When driving in the city, it is crucial that drivers have the ability to search, scan, interpret, and decide on actions in response to traffic. Instruction and experience with city driving—whether actual or simulated—is vital.

In city driving, it is particularly important that students be aware of their driving environment. Knowing when and where to look, maintaining a safety zone, and being aware of potential hazards posed by pedestrians and parked vehicles are valuable skills for the city driver. Drivers should also be able to maintain safe and legal speed and lane positioning, know how to turn safely from one type of street onto another, and communicate with other drivers. Driver education programs, regardless of the type of community in which they are located, should provide students with instruction and experiences to prepare them to drive in urban areas.

Objectives	The student should be able to • describe common conflicts for right and left turns • identify clues for the presence of parked cars, pedestrians, bicyclists, railroad crossings, emergency vehicles • recognize legal and safety considerations of passing on the right • demonstrate an understanding of right-of-way rules and parking lot conflicts • demonstrate basic skills, judgment, and safe attitude for operating a vehicle in busy, complex traffic • demonstrate proper lane choice and positioning on multiple-lane and one-way streets • identify one-way streets through direction of traffic flow, signs, markings • execute correct lane position at intersection and track a proper path • identify and respond to right-of-way situations and turning conflicts • respond to emergency vehicles
Content	• following other cars and trucks—looking ahead, turns and sudden stops, looking away safely, being followed, dealing with tailgating, meeting oncoming traffic, approaching vehicle crosses center line • strategies for driving in city traffic • visual awareness • location of and anticipating traffic signals • adjusting speed and covering the brake pedal • passing and being passed on both sides • turning lanes • entering and leaving one-way streets and boulevards • special lanes (for example, bike, bus, carpool)
Student Activities	• Students attend local traffic court and describe the judicial procedure. • Invite a traffic engineer to the class to explain his or her role in traffic safety. • Demonstrate or have students explain the two second following distance rule. • Students speculate as to why vehicles might cross the center line.

Limited Access Driving

One of the best examples of roadway safety engineering in the HTS is the limited access roadway. The elimination of intersections and control of access allows larger numbers of vehicles to travel at greater speeds more safely and efficiently. Novice drivers who have developed the skills necessary to operate on such roads will be better users of the HTS.

Though traffic flow and access are two major safety factors, often times traffic speed, density, and environmental conditions complicate limited access driving. If students learn to maintain safe and efficient speeds and following distances, they will be one step closer to preventing collisions on limited access roadways.

Objectives	The student should be able to • identify and explain traffic signs of the limited access roadway • explain exit signs and the placement of signs on the interstate highway • identify roadway safety engineering factors of limited access roads and highways • demonstrate procedure for entering and leaving limited access roadways • demonstrate high speed passing and being passed • identify limited access highway hazards • explain why the expressway is the safest driving environment • identify types of freeway interchanges, their use, and conflicts • discuss strategies for lane use and special problems such as tolls, disabled traffic, and construction • define velocitation, highway hypnosis, road blockage, passing, and bunching • demonstrate a margin of safety with other traffic
Content	• entering, blending safely and smoothly, exiting limited access roadways • techniques for safe expressway driving • limited access highway signs • passing maneuvers • lane choice, changing lanes • limited access hazards—missing exit, vehicle break down, construction • cruise control • toll road • design features • types of interchanges—cloverleaf, diamond, directional, trumpet • staying alert—speed hypnosis • judgment of speed and spacing • entrance and exit ramps, timed signal lights • acceleration, deceleration lanes • merging (left or right) • lane selection and position • speed limits (minimum and maximum) • problems—vehicles bunching, blind spots, following and being followed, ramp overflow • crossing traffic • velocitation

Student Activities	• obstacles—disabled vehicles, road construction or repair, toll plazas • Students explain why expressways have lower fatality rates than other highways. • Students diagram types of interchanges and explain how they function. • Students observe an expressway entrance ramp (from a safe location) and identify key behaviors for merging. • Discuss strategies for lane usage, speed, spacing, tolls, disabled cars, signs, or construction. • Demonstrate correct procedure to enter and exit an expressway. • Define terms unique to expressway driving.

Vehicle Safety and Maintenance Checks

Keeping vehicles in safe and efficient operating condition is an important task. Drivers have a responsibility to keep their vehicles safe not only for themselves, but also for those they transport, those they share the roadway with, and society at large.

Driver education programs can provide novice drivers valuable information on maintaining their vehicles. Students should know preventive maintenance procedures, how to select an auto technician, and the value of following a prescribed maintenance schedule. Well maintained vehicles are safer, less expensive to operate, and cause less harm to the environment.

Objectives	The student should be able to • list routine safety and maintenance vehicle checks and service • identify warning lights or other indications that service is due • use an owner's manual to determine maintenance needs for a vehicle • plan a maintenance schedule • change a tire
Content	• need for maintenance or repair—warning lights, interval (mileage or time), signs of malfunction • maintenance and repair—fluid checks, tire pressure and wear, belt and hose checks, fueling a vehicle, oil types, filters, air cleaners, fuses, seasonal preparations • exhaust system and carbon monoxide
Student Activities	• Review recommended maintenance checks in owner's manual. • Check fluids and tire pressure. • Demonstrate a tire change.

Ownership Responsibilities

Owning a motor vehicle carries significant responsibilities; many of these responsibilities are financial. Protecting oneself and others from financial liability is required by law in Wisconsin. Most drivers obtain insurance to meet this requirement. Knowing how to meet financial responsibility requirements can help individuals become careful and informed purchasers of automobile insurance.

Objectives	The student should be able to • explain costs and responsibilities associated with purchasing and maintaining a vehicle and meeting financial responsibility requirements • identify the options for meeting Wisconsin financial responsibility requirements • identify and define insurance terms and apply them to specific situations • identify problems associated with buying, insuring, and maintaining a vehicle as a teenage driver • distinguish "needs" from "wants" when obtaining a vehicle • describe the legal process of selling a car • describe the purpose and nature of insurance • list factors that influence the cost of insurance
Content	• costs, responsibilities, and financial risks of owning a vehicle—vehicle, insurance, taxes, licensing and registration, fuel, repairs and maintenance, tolls, parking fees, miscellaneous expenses • buying versus leasing—options and terms of financing • legal documents • insurance—types, purpose, minimum requirements, factors influencing the cost of insurance • state law • types of insurance coverage—liability insurance, comprehensive insurance, deductible, property damage, bodily injury, collision, un- and under-insured, other riders • selling a vehicle

Motor Vehicles and the Environment

Automobiles extract a heavy price from the environment, so it is appropriate that a program that educates students how to operate automobiles also educate students on the effects of operating those vehicles. In recent years, significant environmental improvements have been made. Unleaded gas is used throughout the United States, drained oils must be properly disposed of, and vehicles manufactured today are in large part recyclable as major manufacturers have become more sensitive to the need to conserve natural resources. Electric or solar power may well provide the fuel for vehicles in the future.

On the down side, however, automobiles are the largest single source of air pollution; autos contribute to global warming through carbon dioxide emissions, to ground-level smog through ozone emissions, to water contamination through run-off from paved surfaces, and to the likelihood of environmental damage through oil drilling, refining, and transporting. And due in large part to dispersed or sprawl-type development, Americans drive more today than ever before. Driver and traffic safety education instructors should inform students about the benefits of carpooling, mass transit, or locating one's residence and job so as to reduce the environmental impact of transportation. Carpooling, for example, cuts hydrocarbon, carbon monoxide, and nitrogen oxide emissions from a typical work commute by 77 percent (American Public Transit Association, 1989). By reducing our dependence on the automobile, we can maintain much of our mobility while limiting heavy environmental costs.

Objectives	The student should be able to • explain the adverse environmental effects of vehicles and ways to reduce these effects • explain vehicle maintenance requirements and their effect on the environment • explain what is meant by alternative fuels • discuss forms of alternative transportation • list federal agencies involved in environmental issues pertaining to motor vehicles • explain methods for disposing of various vehicle fluids and parts to reduce adverse effects on the environment • explain environmental considerations relevant to the purchase of a vehicle • discuss factors influencing gas mileage • list recyclable automotive fluids and identify proper recycling procedures • list disposal procedures for battery, airbag, tires, vehicle • explain fuel efficient acceleration and braking techniques • identify agencies and laws governing disposal of hazardous material
Content	• purchasing a vehicle—fuel type, fuel efficiency, recyclability of parts, emissions, size and weight, design, engine size (cylinders and cubic feet), automatic or standard transmission, cruise control, additional equipment • emission requirements • type of fuel and additives—gas, diesel, electric, propane, experimental fuels • gas mileage—tires, oil/fuel/additives, additional equipment (for example, air conditioning, four-wheel drive) • oil—synthetic versus petroleum, weights • tires—type, size, pressure, rotation, alignment

	• other equipment—shades, running boards, toppers, racks • electronics • environmentally responsible maintenance schedule • fluids—air conditioning coolant, refueling, adding oil, leaks • washing car • disposal and disposal locations—anti-freeze, oil, freon, transmission fluid, battery, airbag, tires, vehicle • vehicle and used parts • driving habits—moderate acceleration versus jackrabbit starts, coasting versus heavy braking, closed windows, fuel mileage reduction in high speed, constant speed • alternative modes of transportation—bus, train, area neighborhood programs, bicycles, motorcycles, mopeds, walking • reducing use of automobile—locating housing and work place in proximity, telecommuting, ride-sharing, park and ride lots, car and vanpooling, reducing days-per-week driving, company mandates or incentives (for example, subsidized mass transit passes, free and convenient parking for carpools) • environmental agencies and how they affect motor vehicle transportation—Environmental Protection Agency (EPA), Department of Natural Resources (DNR), Department of Transportation (DOT)
Student Activities	• Research state and federal laws on disposal of vehicle fluids and materials. • Contact and develop a list of local disposal centers. • Develop a list of local public transportation. • Identify environmental maintenance for family vehicle.

Trip Preparation and Personal Safety/Security

Planning a safe trip requires more than knowing where to go and how to get there. Novice drivers probably have not had the experience of planning a trip. Trip preparation, when done thoroughly, takes into account an array of items that require advance planning. For example, how many novice drivers consider nutritional aspects of their meals while on a trip? How many plan a budget that includes lodging, meals, and recreation or leisure activities? How many notify mail and newspaper carriers to hold delivery in their absence? How many notify neighbors or other family members how and where to make contact? Trip preparation, when done properly and completely, is an extensive process. Simulated trip preparation activities in a driver education program can provide valuable learning opportunities.

Objectives	The student should be able to • use a road map to find a certain location, determine estimated number of miles to destination, and determine best routes to destination • explain a map legend and scale • develop and conduct a pre-trip vehicle preparation checklist • calculate vehicle fuel mileage on a trip • explain how to pack a vehicle efficiently

	• describe safety precautions that should be followed when packing a vehicle or trailer for a trip • identify emergency equipment to include on a trip • plan for the security of the home when preparing for an extended trip • identify someone who will be aware of the family's whereabouts during a trip • describe techniques to ensure maximum safety of vehicle and personal belongings throughout a trip • assist in route planning and in determining expected expenses of fuel, lodging, and food as part of a trip budget • explain procedures and considerations of pulling and backing a trailer • explain what to do when being followed • explain procedures necessary to protect oneself when stranded and in need of help • list the checks necessary before leaving or re-entering a parked vehicle • explain why driving alone or driving at night is potentially dangerous • describe vehicle security devices
Content	• local travel, short trips, long trips • time allocation • time of travel • weather and traffic reports • vehicle checks • route selection • emergency equipment—flashlight, tire jack, lug wrench, spare tire, tire gauge, fire extinguisher (A-B-C type), flares or reflectors, spare fuses, additional fluids (oil, anti-freeze, windshield washer fluid), first aid kit, battery jumper cables, tool kit, and, in winter—tire chains or snow tires, blankets and extra clothing, boots, high energy food, snow shovel, tow line, sand or cat litter for traction, ice scraper, snow brush • planning ahead • map reading—legend, scale, mileage chart, colored symbols, locating town and cities, route selection, estimating mileage and travel time • estimating expenses • determining lodging arrangements • personal preparation—change for tolls and phone calls, map or atlas, spare set of keys, note in vehicle listing destination and phone numbers in case of accident, monies (cash, traveler's checks, or credit cards), telephone numbers for emergency aid and road reports • vehicle loading • visibility • towing techniques • personal safety and security—traveling alone, entering and leaving vehicle, stranded and in need of help, traveling at night, being following • security devices—passive and active systems, factory installed or after-market installation, permanent or portable
Student Activities	• Plan, map out, and calculate expenses for a given trip. • Find current newspaper or magazine articles on personal safety and new security systems.

Instructional Considerations: Simulation

Simulation is an excellent form of supplemental instruction when it is used to enhance students' driver education experiences. Instructors using simulation need to be aware of some special considerations to take full advantage of this instructional format. This section presents considerations for teaching with simulation and for maintaining simulation equipment. Prior to providing simulation instruction, instructors should know about

- teaching techniques that can be incorporated into instruction to enhance simulation instruction,
- the equipment and its operating and maintenance requirements, and
- the films and their contents.

Enhancing Simulation Instruction

Simulation is not a replacement for an active instructor. In simulation instruction, as with all teaching, in order to maximize instruction and student learning, teachers need to plan appropriately.

In order to maximize the benefit of simulation instruction, teachers should

- plan seating locations so that tall students are seated to the rear of the room;
- move away from the control panel in order to see students and the simulation film, and to be visible to students;
- replay certain film segments;
- develop questions and questioning techniques;
- identify drills that might be used to supplement simulation;
- use alternative media (for example, slides, overhead transparencies, videos of local driving scenes, charts, or diagrams) to supplement simulation; and
- allow time for discussion or "processing" of the simulation experience.

Operating and Maintaining Simulation Equipment

As with any piece of technical equipment, proper operation and regular maintenance of simulation equipment is essential. Districts typically enter into a maintenance service contract or use local personnel trained to maintain the equipment. Instructors can aid the maintenance process by performing preventive maintenance on an ongoing basis. Instructors should

- maintain adequate humidity levels (for example, use a humidifier during winter months, and a dehumidifier in the summer);
- maintain normal temperature levels;
- ask students to remove pens, pencils, and other sharp objects from their pockets;
- request that students buckle simulator unit belts after each lesson;

- require students to enter and exit the simulator units only from the prescribed side;
- prevent students from pressing against the dashboard as they enter the simulator units;
- prohibit beverages near the simulator units and instructor control panel;
- establish a sense of equipment ownership;
- establish rules for the operation and use of simulation equipment;
- communicate closely with other teachers who use the facility or simulation equipment; and
- have films cleaned and lubricated, and have the films' emulsion rejuvenated annually.

Regular maintenance will increase the equipment's life span and increase the district's return on investment. When equipment is rented or leased, maintenance contracts are often built into the agreements—at least for the first year. When considering the purchase of a service maintenance contract, one should determine service frequency and the availability of emergency service.

The film library is an essential component of simulation instruction. A strong simulation facility will have a well maintained library of current or regularly updated films. In order to maximize the instructional benefits of the films, instructors should

- preview every film to become familiar with the contents and objectives;
- develop lesson plans, including freeze-frame locations and potential questions; and
- drive through each simulation film to become familiar with it from the student driver's standpoint.

Selection of films will depend on a number of local factors. Those regions that don't have snow can provide experiences in snow and snowy conditions through simulation. For districts without convenient access to an interstate or limited access highway, simulation can offer a way to present such driving environments.

Local districts and instructors can determine their own sequencing of simulation films. In order to determine sequencing, instructors should consider

- the local program's scheduling style (block or concurrent),
- the quantity and content of on-street and classroom lessons, and
- the district's geographic location and proximity to various driving environments.

Assessing Student Performance

There are several approaches available for assessing student simulation performance, including the master control panel's student response record, other assessment instruments such as written essays, tests, and quizzes, and instructor observation of students' transfer of learning.

Instructors may wish to exercise caution in the value placed on scores from the simulator's automatic response recording system. It is important to consider that students are not being taught to drive a simulator, but are developing skills to safely operate a motor vehicle. It has even been suggested that teachers not use simulation for grading purposes. Paper and pencil tests or quizzes also may be of limited value for assessing student simulation performance. Instead, teachers can use the master control panel to respond to students' actions in specific situations.

Careful instructor observation of students will provide more useful information than written test scores. Because simulation is heavily geared toward visual and perceptual rather than manipulative skills development, the most valuable performance assessments are those that consider whether a student successfully transfers learning to the in-car portion of training. If transfer is not observed, modifications can be made to the simulation instruction methodology.

Instructional Considerations: On-Street Driving Instruction

The on-street driving phase of driver education is the most anticipated by students. For many, it symbolizes the near completion of the program and brings them a step closer to driver's license eligibility. On-street driving is, as mentioned earlier, a required component of any complete program of instruction. Depending on the local program and how students are scheduled, many students will have either completed the classroom phase or be concurrently participating in the classroom phase when they start on-street driving.

On-street driving gives students the opportunity to demonstrate their abilities to apply the knowledge they acquired in the classroom phase of instruction. It should include experience driving in different traffic conditions, practice in manipulative skills, and the application of driving strategies learned in the classroom. Students should apply visual perceptual skills as well as the manipulative skills of controlling a vehicle's speed, position, and direction.

Supplemental practice under the guidance of a parent or other adult should be encouraged once behind-the-wheel instruction has begun.

Guidelines

The teacher must be certified by the DPI and use a properly equipped and insured dual-control vehicle. Students are required to have an instruction permit, which should be carried with them whenever they drive. Instructors should record instruction permit information, including the number, date of expiration, and any individual restrictions. In the event that more than 13 months have passed from the time a student completes the classroom to the start of on-street driving, schools are required to provide an additional ten hours of supplemental instruction.

Locally planned lessons can
- strive to enhance the connection between the phases of driver education,
- help students progress from simple to more complex tasks, and
- facilitate a shift from learning procedures for controlling and operating a vehicle to knowing and understanding the process of driving.

Supplemental practice under the guidance of a parent or other adult should be encouraged once behind-the-wheel instruction has begun.

Parents can schedule the student for the state driving test at any time after the student has completed the program.

Content

The content presented in the on-street driving portion of a driver education program depends on a number of factors, including
- the amount of on-street instruction;
- the program's geographic location and accessibility to certain types of conditions, roads, or environments; and
- the content and skills taught in other laboratory phases of the program.

Programs conducted only during the normal school day rarely have the opportunity to provide on-street driving during hours of darkness. In these cases, parents should be encouraged to offer supplemental practice driving sessions to provide students with driving experience after dark.

Advanced or emergency skills can be taught with minimal risk using off-street areas. Many on-street driving instructors incorporate emergency driving skill instruction in some on-street lessons when safe areas can be found. For example, off-road recovery may be incorporated into a rural driving lesson in a location with an adequate shoulder and little traffic. Though there are arguments for and against incorporating advanced or emergency driving skills during on-street driving instruction, local districts must make their own decision whether to include such instruction.

Scheduling

When scheduling on-street instruction, a number of factors need to be considered, including
- number of students and instructional hours required;
- number of lessons and their length;
- scheduling concurrently with classroom instruction or as a block program;
- local scheduling policies (based on age or class level, for example);
- availability of students, vehicles, and instructors; and
- cost of vehicles (when leased on a daily basis).

Local administrators must address these factors in light of their own situations. Many districts conduct on-street driving only outside normal school hours, whereas others provide on-street driving during school hours only, and still others only in the summer. Of course, the most cost efficient instruction may not yield the highest quality instruction. For example, a schedule designed to have students finish on-street instruction in as short a period of time as possible may not allow sufficient time for supplemental practice with parents or other adults. Yet this supplemental supervised experience is essential for young drivers to further develop the skills they acquire during on-street instruction. A brief on-street instruction period may also limit transfer of knowledge and skills from classroom or lab to on-street driving.

On-street lessons should be carefully planned, with each lesson's content and objectives clearly identified. Instructors should schedule

The most cost efficient instruction may not yield the highest quality instruction.

anywhere from two to four students per group. Below are some examples for scheduling different groups of students based on the number of phases of instruction offered and minimum instructional hours required.

A two-phase program (that is, a program based on classroom and on-street driving instruction alone) could use the following schedule for a group of three students:
- one hour lessons—each student drives for 20 minutes and observes for 40 minutes (requires 18 lessons)
- one and one-half hour lesson—each student drives for 30 minutes and observes for 60 minutes (requires 12 lessons)
- two hour lessons—each student drives for one hour and observes for two hours (requires six lessons)

Lessons

Options for planning and conducting on-street lessons include prescribed routes for each lesson, skill area driving, traffic flow environments, or destination driving. Many programs use a combination of these lesson types. Whatever technique local program staff choose, they should strive to include as many different driving environments and conditions as possible so each student is taught a complete set of skills and driving strategies. Regardless of the form of instruction used, instructors should plan on-street instruction to help students achieve the stated objectives.

Prescribed Route Planning

Under prescribed route planning, routes are prepared for every lesson. Careful planning is essential to provide driving experiences that match every content item in the lesson. The use of prescribed routes has several advantages and disadvantages.

Advantages of prescribed route planning include the following:
- All students are taught in a consistent fashion. (This is critical when several instructors teach on-street driving.)
- All students experience the same driving environments and are required to perform the same maneuvers.
- Specific skills are developed for each lesson.
- Both static and dynamic situations can be included. (Static situations are those that will not change, whereas dynamic situations do change.)
- It is easier to locate instructors and students in the event of an emergency.
- It can be easier to maintain a prescribed time frame for lessons.

Disadvantages of prescribed route planning include the following:
- Instructors may become bored by traveling the same route.
- Initial preparation and planning takes time.
- Given students' differing needs and learning styles, not all students will be ready to move on to more advanced techniques at the same time.
- Routes become publicly known, thus increasing the likelihood of harassment by others.
- Unexpected delays could affect whether the route can be completed.

Skill Area Driving

In skill area driving, the instructor knows what subject matter should be provided in each lesson. However, instead of following a prescribed route, instructors can have students drive in areas where certain conditions are available.

Destination Driving

Destination driving is used to assess students' ability to determine their own route to a prescribed location. In destination driving, students select their path of travel, often times without coaching from the instructor. The instructor observes the driver's behaviors and reactions to driving conditions. Upon completion of the activity, the instructor provides feedback based on those observations.

Further Suggestions

- Most on-street instruction should begin in an off-street or light traffic area and progress to more congested areas. Instruction should begin with simple tasks before advancing to more complex tasks.
- Instructors may need to simulate certain conditions that are not available in their area. However, safety for the driver, passengers, and other roadway users must always be considered and never put in jeopardy.
- Development of an on-street driving guide, in-car lesson introductions, demonstrations, and reviews will help facilitate the learning process. The use of a local driving guide also helps assure consistency of instruction when more than one instructor provides on-street instruction.
- Instructors need to be positioned so they can take control of the vehicle if necessary. It is important that instructors test vehicle brakes prior to each lesson. Instruction should be free of in-car distractions that may jeopardize safety. The car radio, for example, may distract some drivers.
- Student commentary driving helps instructors determine what a driver is seeing and thinking. Verbal cues should be used by the instructor, progressing to questioning techniques, and ultimately to instructor observation and evaluation as the student gains proficiency.
- Instructors should offer a review and suggestions for improvement following each lesson. Comments should be professional in nature and presentation.
- Each lesson should have specific objectives. Instructors should develop observation-based assessment of student driving and provide assessments to students and their parents on an ongoing basis.
- Among rules to consider are the following: Students should never be instructed to do something that is illegal or unsafe. Instructors should never drive alone with a student. All students must have their instruction permit in their possession in order to receive driving instruction. And all passengers of the driver education vehicle must use occupant restraints at all times.
- Instructors should designate locations and times to meet students at the start and finish of lessons. This information should be communicated to

parents and guardians. Instructors should avoid making exceptions to this policy unless school administrators approve of those exceptions.
- Parental and adult involvement is an important supplement to the preparation of novice drivers. A supplemental practice driving guide will help parents know what is being taught, and how, why, and what they might do to help the student learn through supervised driving practice.
- Instructors need to realize that their own driving behaviors, whether behind the wheel of a driver education vehicle or their own personal vehicle, are closely observed. Instructors should strive at all times to be positive role models.

Instructional Considerations: Range

The purpose of multiple-vehicle range instruction is to provide students with driving experiences to promote the acquisition of manipulative and perceptual skills. Activities presented in this phase should complement overall program objectives.

Content

Since multiple-vehicle range instruction emphasizes manipulative skill development, range exercises are designed to give students the opportunity to develop those skills. As always, local programs can best determine which skills to include in their program, taking into consideration the size of the facility and the amount of range instruction each student will receive. Sample lesson plans are provided in *The Multiple Car Method* (Automotive Safety Foundation, 1967).

The number of range lessons provided will depend on the content, the type of range facility, the number of vehicles available, and the length of each lesson. Lessons normally involve students driving for 30 to 60 minutes.

Some range instruction may include conflict avoidance skills, such as evasive steering, controlled braking, and tire blowout and skid recovery exercises. This instruction is considered more advanced, and districts need to determine whether these exercises should be included.

Lesson Introductions

The first step to achieve educational objectives and performance goals is to introduce students to the range activity prior to each lesson. Students can prepare through
- printed materials, such as a copy of rules and expectations, instructions, a handbook covering range exercises, or a diagram of the range and exercises;
- visual presentations (using overhead transparencies, video tapes, magnetic board, slides, films, flannel boards, charts/diagrams, and the like); and
- demonstrations of exercises on the range itself.

Further Suggestions

Instructors should consider the following suggestions to enhance range instruction and student learning:
- Use clear, concise, and precise directions.
- Avoid use of terms and phrases that have double meanings.
- Preface all commands by announcing "all vehicles" or by referring to a specific vehicle by number.
- Limit directions to essentials. If a specific driver needs assistance, communicate to that individual in person rather than through the general communication device.
- Be aware of the facility's trouble spots, and position instructors or assistants accordingly. Instructors should always be placed in a safe location and with a good view of the range.
- Make special arrangements for students who need assistance or those having difficulties.
- Avoid using the general communication device to relay criticism; instead, communicate feedback in person.
- Keep records of each student's activities and share those records with on-street instructors.
- Arrange the exercises so they progress from simple to complex. Before allowing students to advance from one level of difficulty to another, ensure that they have demonstrated the ability to conduct more basic exercises.
- Enforce minimum following distances.

A few rules will help ensure the safety of students, instructional personnel, and vehicles. Rules should include maximum speeds, minimum following distances, use of communication devices, and emergency procedures.

Assessing Student Performance

Assessments should be designed to evaluate student skills. Local driver education instructors can take advantage of several instruments that have been developed for incorporation into range programs. Some instruments, for example, rely on awarding points, or point demerits, for observed actions or behaviors.

For example, a range test could assign demerit points for touching cones, crossing pavement lines, having to readjust vehicle position during an exercise, or failing to signal or execute prescribed manipulative techniques. Walter Gray of the Driver and Traffic Safety Instructional Demonstration Center at Indiana State University developed a scoring system in which demerits of seven or 11 points are assessed for driver errors. For example, touching a cone carries a demerit of 11 points. Any time a student has to reposition the vehicle during an exercise, seven demerit points are assessed. If a student fails to attain a certain score, additional range instruction is required. Once a student achieves a certain test score, the student is eligible for on-street instruction. Of course, this policy would not be possible for those programs offering range and on-street instruction concurrently.

Following is an example of a performance-based evaluation based on the specific skill being evaluated. Districts are encouraged to examine their student evaluation methodologies, and to consider using objective evaluations based on student performance.

■ Sample Evaluation

Student Performance Criteria

Exercise	*Performance indicators*
Lane changing	• signal • head check • smooth lane transfer • signal cancellation
T-exercise	• signal • head check • hand-over-hand steering entering exercise • center front target cone in middle of vehicle • stop short of front target cone (within 12 inches) • shift to reverse • correct body positioning for straight-line backing • center rear target cone in middle of vehicle • stop short of rear target cone (within 12 inches, looking back until fully stopped) • shift to drive • hand-over-hand steering to position for exiting exercise • correct signal • hand-over-hand steering exiting exercise • entering traffic flow • lane position in traffic • cancellation of signal
Figure 8	• hand-over-hand steering • vehicle does not touch lane line or leave lane
X-exercise	• hand-over-hand steering forward and reverse • backing in both right and left directions • center front and rear target cones, stopping within 12 inches • look over shoulder until fully stopped
Garage exercise	• signal (enter and exit from street) • hand-over-hand steering • center the vehicle front target cone • body backing positioning • exit garage and enter traffic • lane positioning after backing out of driveway onto street

Y-turn	- signal - positioning vehicle to right side of roadway - left turn signal - hand-over-hand steering to left - stop short of left side curb - place vehicle in reverse - head checks - signal prior to backing - body positioning for maneuvering in reverse - look back until fully stopped - shift gears - traffic flow head checks (left and right) - signal - smooth acceleration - lane positioning
Angle parking (45 degree and perpendicular)	- signal prior to entering - lane positioning - front left and rear right tire tracking - center vehicle in relationship to target cone - stop short of target cone (within 12 inches) - shift to reverse - signal - body positioning for backing out of stall - rear right and front left vehicle tracking - lane positioning in traffic after backing out - shift to drive
Parallel parking	- signal (right or left pending one- or two-way street) - vehicle positioning in reference to vehicle in front of desired parking stall (two to three feet away, back bumpers even) - shift to reverse - head checks and body positioning for backing - hand-over-hand steering - vehicle positioning in stall relative to distance from curb (within 12 inches) and vehicles ahead and behind (minimum of three feet)
Hill parking	- signal and head checks - vehicle distance from curb (within 12 inches) - steering of front wheels (always away from the middle of the road unless uphill with a curb) - application of parking brake - shift to park - signal and head checks - shift into drive - head checks - parking brake release and acceleration - another head check - signal cancellation and positioning in lane

References

American Public Transit Association. *Mass Transit: The Clean Air Alternative.* Washington, DC: American Public Transit Assn., 1989.

Automotive Safety Foundation. *The Multiple Car Method.* Washington, DC: Automotive Safety Fdtn., 1967.

Highway Users Federation for Safety and Mobility. *The Driving Simulator Method.* Washington, DC: Highway Users Fedn. for Safety and Mobility, 1970.

Kolstad, James L. "The ABCs for Teen Drivers." *Car and Travel* Jan.-Feb. 1996, p. 4.

National Highway Traffic Safety Administration. *Fatal Accident Reporting System 1990: A Review of Information on Traffic Crashes in the United States.* Washington, DC: U.S. Dept. of Transportation, 1990.

Wisconsin Department of Transportation. *1991 Wisconsin Traffic Crash Facts.* Madison: WDOT, 1991.

_____. *1994 Wisconsin Traffic Crash Facts.* Madison: WDOT, 1994.

Integration with School and Community 4

Integration within Curriculum
Integration with Other Health Programs
Integration Beyond the Classroom
References

High school students in River Falls, Wisconsin, dedicated this "Light of Life" sculpture in memory of a classmate killed in an automobile crash.
Reprinted by permission, St. Paul Pioneer Press.

Young drivers are influenced by a number of factors outside of the formal driver education curriculum.

Quality driver and traffic safety education programs do more than simply prepare young teenagers to operate a vehicle and obtain a driver's license. Traffic safety education also influences the development of students' knowledge, character, personal responsibility, decision making skills, and, to a degree, behavior. Many of the concepts and skills taught in driver and traffic safety are present in other health, safety, and prevention programs. These topics can be integrated across the school curriculum and other school or community health-related programs to increase instructional effectiveness.

While driver and traffic safety education is an important component in the preparation of safe and responsible drivers for entry into the highway transportation system, driver education is not enough in itself. Driver education programs can prepare novice drivers with the basic knowledge and skills needed to become safe, responsible drivers and traffic citizens, but instruction does not necessarily translate into safe and responsible behavior. Driving behavior is influenced by more than driver education; young drivers are influenced by a number of factors outside of the formal driver education curriculum and classroom, including the larger school environment and the community as a whole.

This chapter discusses curriculum integration across the school curriculum and other health-related programs. It is hoped that this chapter will help local instructors, administrators, and other curriculum staff recognize the role and value of driver and traffic safety education in a comprehensive and integrated health- and safety-related program.

Integration within Curriculum

As previously mentioned, concepts and skills taught through driver and traffic safety education are often related to, and can be integrated across the school curriculum. Examples that will be discussed include such subject areas as math, science, health, social studies, and consumer-related courses.

Math

Whether in driver education or math, students can be provided driving-related learning experiences using math. Instructors can develop traffic safety situations or problems that require the application of mathematics skills. Converting miles per hour to kilometers per hour or gallons of fuel to liters of fuel, calculating fuel efficiency ratios of different cars, planning a budget for a family trip, calculating distances between various locations on a map, using map scales, or calculating short and long term costs of an OWI conviction are examples of exercises involving mathematics skills.

Science

Natural laws are often taught in science courses. Driver and traffic safety education programs also deal with natural laws and their effects on vehicle control. Topical areas include the effects of a vehicle's weight and speed on the force of impact in the event of collision; gravity and its relationship to vehicle traction; effects of vehicle speed, tire tread, and tire pressure on hydroplaning; and friction, traction, and the effects of roadway surface conditions on vehicle control.

Health

Health education, developmental guidance, family and community education, and driver and traffic safety education are several disciplines within schools that focus specifically on the health and safety of students. The potential for integration among these disciplines is significant. Safe and responsible decision making about one's own health and safety is inherent in everyone's daily lives. Such behavior transcends all of these disciplines—whether involving safety belt use, eating habits, or AOD use. Integration across subjects helps students connect learning from one subject to another and results in learning that is more likely to translate into behavior and practice.

Social Studies

Transportation and traffic safety-related content can be integrated quite effectively into social studies courses. Psychology courses, for example, often deal with how and why people behave as they do. In such courses, risk and risk taking behavior can be integrated into discussions of personality or behavior. Social studies courses that address social issues such as legal systems, legislation, and other methods of social control can include examples of traffic control and management. The study of social and legal public policy can include a review of traffic safety legislation involving maximum speed limits, minimum drinking age laws, BAC indicating intoxication, and legislation affecting novice drivers (zero tolerance or graduated licensing, for example).

Consumer-Related Courses

Courses that relate to consumer education can integrate driver and traffic safety education content. One example would involve students determining the effects of different down payment levels, interest rates, and loan periods when purchasing a new or used vehicle. Another valuable topic would be the study of how to shop for auto insurance, factors that affect auto insurance costs, and decisions individuals can make to minimize premium payments yet ensure sufficient coverage. Some consumer-related courses might explore how to properly maintain a vehicle, including how to select a competent and fair auto technician.

Integration with Other Health Programs

In addition to integration within and across a school's curriculum, schools can integrate positive traffic safety attitudes, values, and concepts with other health, safety, and prevention programs.

This section will discuss avenues that schools might consider in their efforts to provide programs that promote safe, healthy behavior and prevent or reduce youth involvement in high risk behavior. This discussion will include a framework that schools can use to structure their prevention and wellness program.

School Efforts in Youth Development

Though many young people are involved in high risk behavior or situations that increase their level of risk, most are resilient enough to avoid serious long term consequences. Resiliency consists of those self-righting tendencies that are inherent in human development. A growing body of research supports school involvement in prevention, positive youth development, and resiliency training.

Most schools have programs to promote healthy and safe behaviors and positive youth development. Unfortunately, these programs may operate without coordination and in isolation of each other. In some instances, programs duplicate efforts, using resources that could have been delivered more efficiently and effectively through coordination and integration.

A growing body of research on youth risk behaviors, prevention programming, and positive youth development has helped schools develop more effective programming in these areas. Research indicates, for example, that there are relationships between certain high risk behaviors. If a student is identified as having a problem in one area, there is often a high degree of likelihood that the student is also at risk in another area. A review of this phenomenon, referred to as co-occurrence of risk behavior, follows.

Co-occurrence of Risk Behavior

Researchers have used surveys to provide snapshots of youth at given periods of time. Some surveys identify and track specific types of youth behaviors that are closely linked to student health and well being. One such survey of 47,000 students in 25 states was conducted by Peter Benson of the Search Institute. Benson's study recommends, among other things, that parents, educators, community leaders, and individuals become involved in youth-serving organizations. For educators specifically, the report suggests prevention programs in multiple areas of risk, including alcohol, tobacco, illegal drugs, depression and suicide, sexuality, and vehicle safety. In addition, the study evaluated correlations of at-risk behaviors.

Figure 1 identifies patterns of co-occurrence of risk behaviors and calculates the probability that a student at risk in one area is also at risk in other areas. For example, if a student is at risk in alcohol use, then there is an 86 percent chance that she or he is at risk in vehicle safety. Figure 1 illustrates the extent to which an individual who is at risk in an area other than vehicle safety is also likely to be at risk for vehicle safety.

Figure 1

Patterns of Co-occurrence of Risk Behaviors

If At Risk in This Area	Alcohol Use	Tobacco Use	Illicit Drug Use	Sexuality	Depression/ Suicide	Anti-Social Behavior	School	Vehicle Safety
Alcohol Use	—	42%	27%	70%	33%	49%	23%	86%
Tobacco Use	66%	—	35%	77%	39%	53%	26%	85%
Illicit Drug Use	72%	60%	—	84%	46%	61%	32%	88%
Sexuality	49%	34%	22%	—	34%	41%	19%	77%
Depression/ Suicide	41%	30%	21%	59%	—	38%	18%	73%
Anti-Social Behavior	54%	37%	24%	64%	34%	—	22%	82%
School	62%	43%	31%	72%	40%	53%	—	82%
Vehicle Safety	41%	25%	15%	52%	28%	35%	15%	—

From *Search Institute Report: The Troubled Journey*

The study shows that districts emphasizing health and wellness prevention need to consider programs that target multiple risk behaviors and the relationships between high risk behaviors in one area and the likelihood of co-occurrence with other high risk behavior. Since motor vehicle crashes are the leading cause of injury and death for young people, the data support the need for school involvement in traffic safety-related programs and initiatives, including driver education.

Not only do students tend to place themselves in situations of high risk, but, in many instances, they fail to recognize the level of risk. AAA's *Model Curriculum Outline* (1995) indicates that more emphasis should be placed on helping novice drivers perceive and evaluate risks and on motivating them to reduce risk while driving. This also holds true for other high risk behaviors; through curriculum integration, schools can have strong influence on reducing youth involvements in many high risk behaviors. Thus, educating students to be aware of risk is a critical component of the health and wellness mission.

Integration Beyond the Classroom

Most Wisconsin school districts have programs that promote and support the health and well being of students. Many of these programs can be coordinated and integrated to ensure effective delivery. In light of this, the DPI Student Services Prevention and Wellness Team has developed a conceptual framework that integrates prevention, health and wellness, youth development, and resiliency strategies to help districts plan comprehensive, integrated health and wellness programs. The concepts and integrated approach presented in the framework (DPI, 1995) will help districts maximize their use of limited resources while continuing efforts to ensure that each student has maximum opportunity to succeed in school.

The central focus and overall goal of the framework is the development of healthy, resilient, and successful learners. In the framework, learners are nurtured in an environment that addresses the whole person. In order to assist students in becoming successful, healthy, and resilient, the framework presents the following components:

- curriculum, instruction, and assessment;
- pupil services;
- student programs;
- adult programs;
- healthy school environment; and
- family and community connections.

The framework promotes a team approach to develop a continuum of services using multiple strategies to build connections among academic programs, pupil services, youth programs, and the larger learning environment. Connections facilitate networking, cooperation, coordination, and collaboration, all representing different degrees to which programs are integrated. These connections help to eliminate gaps in services and programs for youth in need. The framework provides means for program improvement and a way to develop increased support for driver education and other prevention programs within the school. Ensuring that the traffic safety education program is part of a multi-faceted approach can strengthen a district's overall curriculum and high risk behavior prevention efforts.

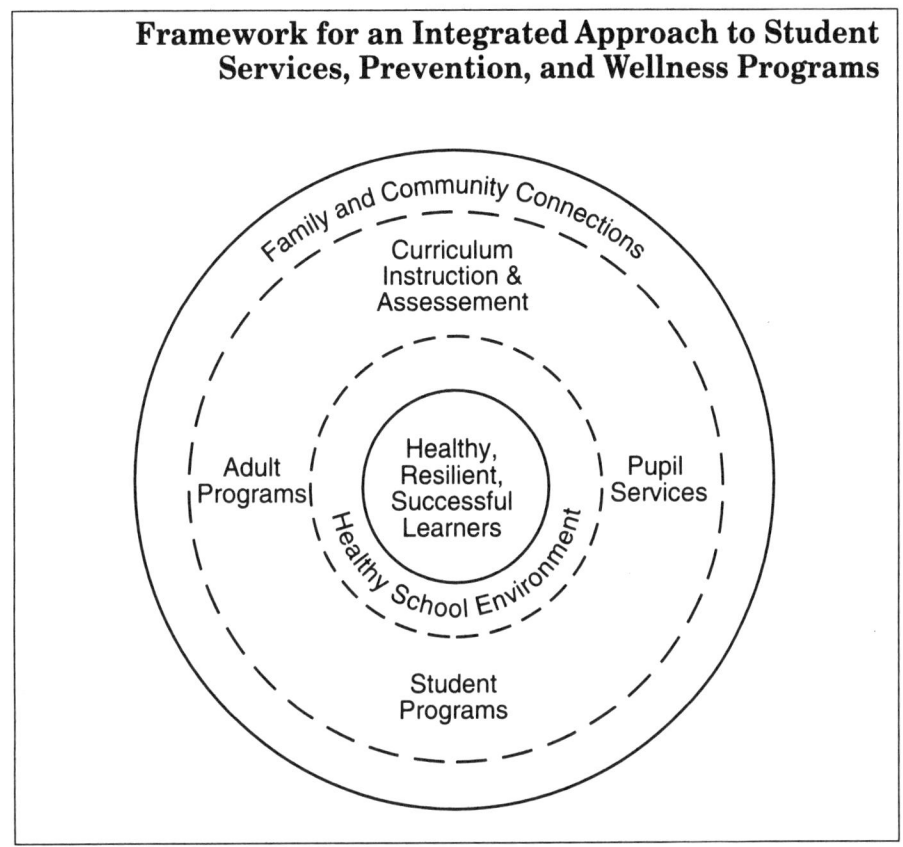

Figure 2

Framework for an Integrated Approach to Student Services, Prevention, and Wellness Programs

(Concentric circles diagram: outer ring "Family and Community Connections"; next ring containing "Curriculum Instruction & Assessement", "Adult Programs", "Pupil Services", "Student Programs"; inner ring "Healthy School Environment"; center "Healthy, Resilient, Successful Learners")

the heart of a quality driver and traffic safety education program is a sound instructional program embedded in a healthy school environment

As mentioned earlier, the heart of a quality driver and traffic safety education program is a sound instructional program embedded in a healthy school environment. The following discussion of driver and traffic safety education is based on the framework components identified above.

Pupil Services

Another avenue for integrating education and prevention efforts is pupil services. A school's existing pupil services infrastructure can be used to augment and reinforce the mission of driver education. Historically, pupil services has been composed of four disciplines: school psychology, social work, counseling, and nursing. Driver education instructors should consider involving pupil services staff for several reasons. Pupil services personnel can help identify at-risk or special needs students and can help provide or identify resources to better meet student needs. Pupil services staff are also often involved in course scheduling, which is a crucial element in the effective delivery of driver education. Finally, pupil service personnel are valuable assets in working with parents and community organizations and are often involved in student assistance programs and other school programs emphasizing student health and safety.

Student Programs

Student programs can serve as a natural extension of a driver and traffic safety education program. Traffic safety programs conducted outside the classroom can promote student involvement in activities to promote health and safety. For example, youth programs emphasizing traffic safety within the school and community can raise the visibility of traffic safety issues through buckle-up campaigns, poster contests, rallies against drunk driving, candlelight vigils, and so on. Such activities can provide students, the school, and the community as a whole with exposure to traffic safety education activities conducted by students themselves.

Student Organizations

Of course, teachers know that student behavior is greatly influenced by peer groups. Rather than allowing peer influences to counteract the lessons students learn in driver and traffic safety education, instructors can take advantage of peer influence to support their educational mission.

Robert Anastas, founder of SADD, believes that when a problem arises within a certain group, the solution can also be found within the group. Anastas was convinced that youth have the power and ability to influence the behaviors of their peers. This conviction led him to start the national SADD organization, which is based on youth empowerment guided by adults.

Two examples of national peer programs whose origins and emphases evolved around traffic safety issues include SADD and NSSP (National Student Safety Program). Each of these national organizations has local chapters throughout the country and sponsor youth safety conferences. The organizations encourage local chapters to become involved in broad youth health, safety, and prevention efforts.

Adult Programs

Adult programs provide information and support to adults who are directly involved in the care and education of students. Motivated adults who promote health and safety play an important positive role in young people's lives. Safe and healthy behaviors on the part of adults reinforce healthy messages from the school curriculum and the school and community environment.

Though society has seen significant changes in the role of families, parents (or guardians) continue to be an important influence in the development of young drivers. Because of this, traffic safety educators need to encourage parent and adult involvement in the instructional program and in the development of young drivers. Educators should inform parents and adults about their programs. It is important, for example, that adults be informed about course content, procedures, and how a responsible adult can supplement instruction through home activities and practice driving sessions.

Parents who take time to develop with their children the rules and responsibilities of driving—as well as actions that will be taken when rules or expectations are not met—help develop responsible drivers. Some examples of adult programs follow.

Role Modeling

The behavior of adults is a powerful influence on youth behavior. Influential adults include not only parents and other adult relatives, but also friends, teachers, neighbors, and others. These adults serve as role models for developing youth. The cliche "do what I say, not what I do," is inappropriate when it comes to role modeling. If an undesirable behavior is prevalent among influential adults, young people are likely to mirror the behavior. At the same time, adults who model positive driving behavior help shape that positive behavior in novice drivers.

The behavior of adults is a powerful influence on youth behavior.

Of course, the traffic safety instructor is also an important role model in determining young driver behavior. Driver education instructors need to be aware that their own behavior as drivers and responsible citizens is under close observation, and that they must always model safe and healthy driving behavior.

Parent Involvement and Parent Programs

There are many ways to promote adult involvement in the mission of driver education. Many programs conduct parent nights, for example. On such occasions, parents are invited to attend an evening session in which instructors inform the parents about the driver education program—its expectations, rules, procedures, and goals. These events may also include a guest speaker or two, a tour of the facility, a question and answer period, and refreshments. However, parental involvement can go far beyond this single event.

Open and ongoing communications is vital to cultivating and encouraging parental involvement. For example, instructors can have periodic telephone conversations with parents, or develop a monthly newsletter for parents. Driver and traffic safety educators can consider some of the following approaches to promote family involvement in the driver and traffic safety education mission:

- Establish a parent's night to
— inform parents about the program.
— share concerns about novice drivers and traffic crashes.
— provide materials describing practice driving lessons and techniques.
— describe how maneuvers are done, explaining why certain steps or procedures are important.
— invite a guest speaker to discuss a topic relevant to parents.

— involve other community agency representatives (for example, insurance representatives, automobile technicians, law enforcement personnel, driving examiners, judges, and so on).
- Develop a parent's driving guide to
— provide parents with suggestions on working with novice drivers.
— indicate how parents can supplement and reinforce the driver education curriculum.
— provide key terms and definitions.
— suggest routes or major skills for parents to emphasize.
- Require a driving log of adult-supervised practice sessions and ask parents and students to
— ensure that the log is signed by the adult and student every time a practice session is conducted.
— include identification of exercises and type of driving environment.
— submit the log for instructor review.
- Encourage parents to discuss their expectations, establish rules, penalties, and rewards, and enforce them. Emphasize that the more monitoring parents do with their children, the better.
- Suggest that parents allow gradually increased driving privileges over time rather than immediate and total privileges from the start. For example, parents might impose curfews, limit the number of passengers in the vehicle, maintain a mileage log to monitor number of miles driven, establish rules as to when the child is allowed to use the vehicle, and decide what operating costs the student will share.
- Encourage parents to be role models of safe, responsible driving behavior.
- Invite parents to ride along during an in-car driving lesson. This not only allows parents to observe the teaching and learning process, it also helps them develop greater confidence to offer supervised practice driving sessions for their children.
- Invite parents to sit in on classroom sessions. Encourage them to become active participants in classroom activities.

Adult programs, especially those that promote the active involvement of parents or guardians, are valuable assets for driver and traffic safety education programs. Not only do such initiatives aid in the educational mission of teaching novice drivers to be safe, responsible members of the HTS, but they help build a strong base of support for the local program; such community support can prove valuable in ensuring the continued presence of quality high school driver education programs.

Healthy School Environment

According to the DPI (1995), a healthy school environment is "the culture and climate that exist within a school that support the physical, mental, emotional, and social well-being and safety of all its members." It is not a program, but rather an atmosphere that is developed through all the experiences that students have in school. The overall environment and attitude affects how, and to a degree why, individuals behave as they do.

The environment, which is shaped by the components shown in the framework, has significant effects on traffic safety education. When people are exposed to environments that are mutually supportive and that encourage healthy choices and behaviors, a favorable climate and attitude is developed and sustained.

There are many factors that affect the environments in which we exist. Unfortunately, many of the influences do not promote healthy behaviors. This is evident in young people's driving behaviors and other high risk behaviors. Developing an environment that promotes health and safety issues remains one of the most significant challenges to professionals in health, safety, and prevention areas.

Family and Community Connections

Successful driver and traffic safety education programs have developed close working relationships with individuals and organizations in the local community. Many driver education teachers are involved in community traffic safety initiatives; likewise, many local business people and professionals are actively involved in traffic safety education classrooms as guest speakers or as contacts on traffic safety topics.

Role of Community

The environment of students goes beyond the school and the family to encompass the wider community in which students live. It is vital that driver and traffic safety educators consider the influence of the community on novice drivers. When a community supports and encourages safe and responsible driving, it is likely that young drivers will develop positive habits. When young people exhibit risk-taking behaviors and members of the community challenge those behaviors, it makes a strong statement that such behaviors are not tolerated within the community.

Developing Community Support

Driver education programs can take advantage of a wide range of community resources to help reinforce their driver and traffic safety mission and to gain greater support within the community. Instructors can bring in guest speakers with expertise in specific content areas, or call on community groups for funds to support youth safety programs, for example. However, in building support for the local driver education program, instructors should realize that school–community interaction is a two-way street; traffic safety instructors can also offer their expertise to the community. Instructors can contribute to their community by making presentations to community organizations, by conducting a driver enrichment program for senior citizens, by conducting a driver training or safety seminar for a local company's drivers, or by serving on government traffic safety committees.

Following is a list of several ways instructors might build on community relations to develop a stronger program and deeper support within the community. Driver and traffic safety educators can

- develop community support by involving community members as guest speakers or as resource contacts for students working on reports or projects.
- offer driver enrichment programs for local companies, conduct senior citizen driver awareness programs, or speak at service organization functions.
- facilitate the involvement of youth traffic safety groups in community service projects, especially projects tied to traffic safety-related functions or activities (for example, taking seat belt surveys, opening doors for younger children at elementary schools or pre-schools, cleaning roadsides, washing windshields at business locations or waysides, conducting fluid checks, and so on).
- conduct field trips in which the class visits traffic courts, police stations, emergency rooms, or insurance companies.
- use their expertise to develop, or have students develop, traffic safety articles for local newspapers. Another possibility would be to develop a radio talk show or series of talk shows around traffic safety issues.
- ask radio and television personalities to provide traffic safety reminders on the air.
- develop driver awareness programs in the community stressing the importance of good role modeling for traffic safety.
- seek organizational sponsorship of students through scholarships or fellowships. Some local organizations might sponsor a student in driver education with the understanding that the student will devote a certain amount of time to that organization or some other community project.
- develop partnerships with employers and other organizations. Employers can help develop traffic safety awareness in the community by providing employees with traffic safety enrichment programs, requiring the use of occupant restraints, or offering incentives for good driving records or for following safety rules and regulations when using company vehicles. Some companies provide employees with a "new baby" reimbursement for purchasing a child restraint seat, for example. Companies can also offer incentives to encourage employees to use mass transit, or bicycle or walk to work.

Driver and traffic safety education can equip students with media literacy skills that enable them to critically analyze media messages.

Role of the Media

The mass media also make up part of the community or environment within which students live and learn. The media play an important role in presenting role models and influencing youth behavior. Driver and traffic safety educators can encourage students to be aware of images presented through the mass media and can help students become more sophisticated and critical as media viewers, readers, and consumers. Driver and traffic safety education can equip students with media literacy skills that enable them to critically analyze media messages.

Advertising is believed to be closely related to high risk behavior. In particular, alcohol and tobacco advertisers have been accused of promoting underage consumption. The motion picture and television industries, for their part, have been criticized for emphasizing violence and aggressive behaviors. That such content influences drivers is not surprising, given the large amount of time youth and adults spend watching television and the frequency with which high speed chase scenes or reckless driving behaviors appear in television shows and movies.

The images put forth in media programming and advertising may have adverse effects on societal health and safety. The AAA Foundation for Traffic Safety has funded reports on the impacts of media and advertising on teenagers. One of the studies (AAA Foundation for Traffic Safety, 1987) examined the impact of beer advertisements on brand recognition among minors. The study noted that marketing techniques were used to attract younger people to a specific brand of beer by creating the perception that alcohol consumption has only positive effects. Driving education instructors, parents, and others who care about the health and well being of young citizens must work to counter the misleading messages and negative influences so prevalent in the mass media.

References

AAA Foundation for Traffic Safety. *Myths, Men, and Beer*. Washington, DC, 1987.

_____. *Novice Driver Education Model Curriculum Outline*. Washington, DC, 1995.

Benson, Peter L. *The Troubled Journey: A Profile of American Youth*. A report published for RespecTeen. Minneapolis: Lutheran Brotherhood. Date unknown.

Wisconsin Department of Public Instruction. *Framework for an Integrated Approach to Student Services, Prevention, and Wellness Programs*. Madison: DPI, 1995.

Issues and Trends 5

Outside Contracting
Instructor Shortages
Graduated Licensing
Advancements in Technology
References

This chapter discusses future trends in driver and traffic safety education. In the future, program administrators may experience a shortage of driver education instructors. Due to teacher shortages and fiscal constraints, programs may be forced to explore alternatives such as outside contracting. Instructors are also likely to confront changes in how instruction is delivered over the coming years. One such change is graduated licensing, a licensing system which involves gradual increases in driving privileges for novice drivers. A second factor that will influence teachers and the teaching process is the increased application of computer technology to driver education. Each of these trends is discussed in some detail in this chapter.

Outside Contracting

Although public school districts are encouraged to maintain their own programs of instruction in driver education, local districts do have authority to contract with certain outside agencies for equipment, materials, or instruction. Programs can, for example, contract with a CESA or TC for driver education services, provided such services and instructional staff meet DPI program standards.

Based on data from 1995-96, of the approximately 388 public schools offering driver education:

- 8.7 percent (36) contract with a CESA or TC for some service and maintain eligibility for categorical aids
- 1.2 percent (5) contract with a CESA only for simulation
- 5.1 percent (21) contract with a CESA for both classroom and lab
- 1.9 percent (8) contract with a TC for both classroom and lab
- 0.5 percent (2) contract with a CESA for only one phase of their program's instruction

Of the estimated 415 public high schools in the state, 27 indicated that they do not offer driver education. This represents about 6.3 percent of the high schools in the state. Thus, Wisconsin continues to be a leader in terms of the percentage of public high schools that offer school-based driver education. The fact that most high schools offer driver education is a strong factor in helping students lead healthy, safe, and productive lives as users of the HTS.

When public schools offer driver education directly through the school, more students have access to consistent, affordable instruction. And because of categorical aid from the state, districts are able to obtain reimbursement to help offset instructional costs. The health of both students and the community in which they live improves when public schools offer driver education programs. Districts structured around health, prevention, and wellness issues according to the *Framework for an Integrated Approach to Student Services, Prevention, and Wellness Programs* (DPI, 1995) can include driver education as a key prevention-related course. Driver education programs devote a significant amount of time to content such as individual responsibility, identification and recognition of risk, and alcohol and other drug issues. Many of the concepts presented in the driver education curriculum cross interdisciplinary boundaries and can support other areas of the curriculum.

In some schools, driver education has been used as an incentive for strong academic performance, or to encourage at-risk students to remain active in school and in extra-curricular activities. Contracting outside of the school for driver education may limit the integration of driver education into the wider curriculum and may hinder program flexibility to respond to changing student and program needs.

Instructor Shortages

As increased numbers of driver education instructors retire, there has been a growing demand for new driver education instructors. The majority of new driver education certification candidates are practicing teachers rather than teachers-in-training. Most of these candidates teach in districts where the existing driver education teacher is ready to retire; by obtaining their driver education teaching license, practicing teachers can obtain the credentials necessary to replace the retiring teacher.

In other cases, districts have seen significant increases in student populations and are in need of additional instructors to assist in the on-street driving portion of their programs. Many of these instructors will be hired on a part-time basis. At the same time, the number of institutions that provide coursework and certification programs in driver education has dwindled. At one time, there were approximately 13 institutions in Wisconsin offering certification programs for driver and traffic safety education teachers or teachers-in-training. In 1996, only two programs remain—at the University of Wisconsin–Whitewater and the University of Wisconsin–Stout.

Teacher certification concerns have also led districts to consider contracting out with CESAs and TCs for driver education services. Though this may temporarily relieve districts of having to hire driver education teachers, it should be noted that TCs and CESAs will also have difficulty finding certified teachers.

In the most recent employment outlook summary, driver education is the field with the most active teachers over the age of 51. Within a few short years, many of these individuals will be retiring. When contrasted with the declining numbers of individuals enrolling in driver education teacher preparation programs, signs point to a possible teacher shortage.

Graduated Licensing

The graduated licensing initiative is likely to have a major impact on driver education. Graduated licensing is currently being explored by the NHTSA. It is based on the idea that young drivers should be phased gradually into full driving privileges. Very simply stated, graduated licensing is a licensing system enabling novice drivers to earn increased driving privileges over time, based on their development of driving skills and increased maturity. A number of organizations have been involved in planning graduated licensing, including the NHTSA, the American Driver and Traffic Safety Education Association, AAA, and the American Association of Motor Vehicle Administrators.

Currently, in most states, when a young driver obtains a driver's license, she or he is allowed full driving privileges. Many of these new drivers have very little driving experience. In fact, a number of them have been provided only minimum instruction through a driver education course, and little, if any, supervised driving with a parent or other adult. Many have little or no experience in driving after dark or in inclement weather conditions.

Graduated licensing, as it is currently envisioned, would involve a three-phase approach to granting driving privileges. The first phase would consist of instruction in the basics of driving, traffic law, and driving strategies. During this period of approximately six months, the student would be allowed to drive with a driver education instructor or an authorized adult only. If, after six months, the individual has maintained a clear driving record and avoided alcohol-related infractions, he or she would be allowed to progress to the second phase.

The second phase of licensure would allow an individual to drive without supervision during specified times of day and with a limited number of passengers. In this phase, the driver and all passengers would be required to use occupant restraints. The driver would not be allowed to drive after certain hours of the day unless accompanied by a properly licensed adult. Drivers would obtain further instruction in driver education, dealing especially with decision making, risk, risk perception, driving strategies to reduce conflicts, and adverse behaviors that affect driving. This second phase would last for 12 months, and if, upon the end of the 12 months the driver maintains a clear driving record, including no AOD-related infractions, she or he would be allowed to proceed to the third phase—full driving privileges. Those not progressing to the next stage would repeat the previous stage in order to receive additional training.

One can only speculate as to how graduated licensing might affect high school driver education programs. One possibility is that graduated licensing may result in partnerships between public schools and commercial driving schools, in which formal classroom education would be provided by the public schools and in-car instruction by private, commercial driving schools.

It is thought that a graduated licensing system would have a positive effect on novice driver crash involvement. Significant improvements have been reported for countries having similar graduated licensing programs. Currently, more than a dozen states have some aspect of graduated licensing in their licensing procedures. Wisconsin's probationary license, for example, reflects the philosophy of graduated privileges. In Wisconsin, novice drivers first receive a probationary driver's license.

Once the driver maintains an acceptable driving record for two years, he or she is issued a regular driver's license.

Advancements in Technology

Advancements in computer and information technology have changed the way people live their lives. Few can disagree that technology will continue to result in changes—this is as true in driver and traffic safety education as in other fields.

No one can be sure how technology and technological advancements will affect the future of driver education programs. However, many believe that technology will have a significant impact on how driver education instruction is delivered. Therefore, it is critical that teachers continue to develop their computer skills and keep current in technological resources as they are developed.

Technology will play a significant role in how driver education programs change and improve. Though not an end in itself, technology can be incorporated in ways that improve instruction and student learning.

Software Developments

The AAA Foundation for Traffic Safety Research and NHTSA are taking an active interest in computer technology in the area of driver and traffic safety, including its use in novice driver education programs. Many believe that self-paced computer software learning packages have great potential for supplementing current forms of instruction and for improving student motivation and learning.

Software developers continue to develop affordable driver and traffic safety-related software for programs and for individual students. In light of continued growth in the number of families owning a computer, and an increase in the number of people with computer skills, more individual learning packages are likely to be developed. Graduated licensing and the desire for increased use of computer technologies are likely to accelerate this process.

There is little doubt that technology is the most significant factor influencing how educators will teach and students will learn in the future. Driver education programs today are confronted with limits on instructional hours and resources. Technology may provide techniques to expand student learning experiences inside and outside the classroom despite limited resources.

Application of Technology

Personal computers and software have been incorporated into existing driver education programs to a significant extent. Below are examples of how computer technology has influenced driver and traffic safety education programs.

Computer technology has been used in driver education administrative tasks in the following ways:
- class registration
- scheduling
- grading
- generating letters and reports
- record retention and retrieval
- test development
- access to traffic safety resources via the Internet, BBSs (bulletin board systems), and on-line services
- electronic communication and information sharing with peers throughout the world

In addition, traffic safety instruction has made use of computer technology. Some examples include
- lesson planning and organization;
- multi-media;
- slides and transparencies;
- automation of presentations;
- student guides;
- development, storage, and retrieval of student assignments;
- self-paced, individual student learning programs; and
- assessments instruments.

References

Wisconsin Department of Public Instruction. *Framework for an Integrated Approach to Student Services, Prevention, and Wellness Programs.* Madison: DPI, 1995.

Appendixes 6

A. *PI 21 of the Wisconsin Administrative Code*
B. *PI 3.13 of the Wisconsin Administrative Code*
C. *Resources*

Appendix A

PI 21 of the Wisconsin Administrative Code

Chapter PI 21
DRIVER EDUCATION PROGRAMS

PI 21.01 Applicability and purpose
PI 21.02 Definitions
PI 21.03 Uniform marking standards
PI 21.04 Minimum standards for department approval under s. 343.06(1)(c), Stats.
PI 21.05 Issuance of Wisconsin driver education certificates
PI 21.06 Driver education aid

PI 21.01 Applicability and purpose. This chapter establishes uniform marking standards for vehicles used as driver education vehicles pursuant to s. 341.267(1)(b), Stats.; establishes minimum standards which all high school driver education programs must meet to obtain department approval under s. 343.06(1)(c), Stats.; establishes standards for issuance of Wisconsin driver education certificates; and establishes minimum standards which driver education programs must meet to be eligible to receive state aid under s. 121.41(1), Stats.
History: Cr. Register, May, 1986, No. 365, eff. 7-1-86.

PI 21.02 Definitions. In this chapter:
(1) "Behind-the-wheel instruction" means that portion of the driver education program in which the student is actually driving a vehicle.
(2) "CESA" means a cooperative educational service agency, under ch. 116, Stats.
(3) "CHCEB" means county handicapped children's education boards, under ch. 115, Stats.
(4) "Classroom instruction" includes both individual or group teaching and learning activities which involve study of the inter-relationship of persons and the motor vehicle within the traffic environment.
(5) "Department" means the department of public instruction.
(6) "Laboratory instruction" means that portion of the program which provides students the opportunity for driving experiences and includes behind-the-wheel instruction, observation instruction, and simulation instruction.
(7) "Multiple-vehicle driving range instruction" or "range instruction" means that portion of the program on which the student is driving a vehicle on a designated off-street facility on which a number of motor vehicles operate simultaneously.
(8) "Observation instruction" means the instruction which occurs during the time a student is a passenger in a vehicle in which another student is receiving behind-the-wheel instruction.
(9) "On-street instruction" means that portion of the program in which a student is driving a vehicle on public streets or highways in a dual-controlled vehicle under the supervision of a driver education teacher, or is a passenger in the vehicle while another student is driving.
(10) "Private school" means an institution which operates a high school level educational program and meets the criteria under s. 118.165(1), Stats. or has been determined to be a private school under s. 118.167, Stats.
(11) "Simulation instruction" means the use of a synthetic training devices to prepare a student for driving a real motor vehicle.

(12) "VTAE" means a vocational, technical and adult education district established under ch. 38, Stats.
History: Cr. Register, May, 1986, No. 364, eff. 7-1-86.

PI 21.03 Uniform marking standards. (1) All motor vehicles used as driver education vehicles in programs operated by public school districts, private schools, CHCEBs, CESAs and VTAEs shall be marked with signs as follows:

(a) The sign inscription shall read STUDENT DRIVER or DRIVER EDUCATION. The letters of the inscription shall be at least 2 inches in height and the inscription shall be visible from the front, back and both sides of the vehicle.

(b) The school shall choose one of the following combinations of size and type of signs:

1. Signs which are at least 9 inches by 18 inches placed on each side of the vehicle, and signs which are at least 6 inches by 12 inches placed on the front and rear of the vehicle;

2. Signs which are at least 9 inches by 18 inches placed on each side of the vehicle, and a 2-sided sign which is at least 9 inches by 18 inches placed on the roof of the vehicle; or

3. A 3-sided sign on which each side is at least 5 inches by 16 inches placed on the roof of the vehicle.

(c) The sign shall be school bus yellow with black lettering.

(2) The markings shall be removed when the vehicle is being operated for other than behind-the-wheel instruction or necessary maintenance and storage.

(3) The school's name shall be on the sign. If the vehicle is a dealer-loan vehicle, the dealer's name may be on the sign. The school's name and dealer's name may be in letters less than 2 inches in height.
History: Cr. Register, May, 1986, No. 365, eff. 7-1-86.

PI 21.04 Minimum standards for department approval under s. 343.06(1)(c), Stats. A public school, private school, CHCEB, or CESA driver education program shall be approved by the department under s. 343.06(1)(c), Stats., if the program uses vehicles which meet the requirements of s. PI 21.03 and the program meets the following requirements:

(1) COURSE STANDARDS.

(a) A driver education course shall include the following:

1. At least 30 hours of classroom instruction,
2. At least 6 hours of observation instruction, and
3. At least 6 hours of actual on-street behind-the-wheel instruction.

a. Multiple-vehicle driving range instruction may be substituted for up to 4 hours of the required 6 hours of on-street instruction using a formula that 2 hours of multiple-vehicle driving range instruction is equivalent to one hour of on-street instruction.

b. Simulation instruction may be substituted for up to 3 hours of the required 6 hours of on-street instruction using a formula that 4 hours of simulation instruction is equivalent to one hour of on-street instruction.

c. When both simulation and range laboratory instruction methods are used, the program must include at least 2 hours of actual on-street behind-the-wheel instruction.

(b) During the regular school year, the classroom course shall extend over at least 6 weeks for each student. During a summer school program, the classroom course shall extend over at least 3 weeks for each student.

(c) The on-street driving instruction shall extend over at least 3 weeks for each student. No student may spend more than one hour per day actually behind-the-wheel in the on-street instruction. The one hour limitation does not include observation instruction.

(2) REFRESHER COURSE. If more than one year and one month elapses between completion of the classroom instruction and commencement of the laboratory instruction, a refresher course of classroom instruction shall be required. The refresher course shall be at least 10 hours, and shall include a course of study deemed appropriate by the school district.

(3) TEACHER REQUIREMENTS. Teachers of the classroom instruction, simulation instruction, range instruction, and on-street instruction shall possess a valid license to teach driver education issued by the department as required in s. PI 3.21(2).

(4) APPROVAL PROCEDURES. A public or private high school, CHCEB, or CESA shall submit its driver education course plan to the department for approval on forms provided by the department. The course may not be taught until the plan is approved. Any proposed change in a course which has been approved by the department shall be submitted to the department for approval prior to its implementation.

Note: Form PI 1709 Driver education program approval, may be obtained from Student Services/Prevention and Wellness Team, Department of Public Instruction, 125 South Webster Street, P.O. Box 7841, Madison, WI 53707.

History: Cr. Register, May, 1986, No. 365, eff. 7-1-86.

PI 21.05 Issuance of Wisconsin driver education certificates. (1) Annually, public school districts, private schools, CHCEBs, and CESAs shall certify to the department the number of students who have satisfactorily completed the approved driver education program.

Note: Form PI 1715 Application for driver education certificates.

(2) The department shall provide a Wisconsin driver education certificate for each student who was certified to have satisfactorily completed the approved driver education program, as provided by s. 343.06(1)(c), Stats.

Note: Form PI 1714 Wisconsin driver education certificate.

(3) In this section, "satisfactorily completed" means the student received a passing grade and participated in at least the required number of hours of instruction as required in s. PI 21.04(1).

History: Cr. Register, May, 1986, No. 365, eff. 7-1-86.

PI 21.06 Driver education aid. (1) To be eligible to receive state aid under the provisions of s. 121.41(1) Stats., a driver education program shall meet the requirements of ss. PI 21.03 and 21.04, and the requirements of this section.

(2) Aids shall be paid for eligible students as defined in sub. (3) who are residents of Wisconsin and who, during the preceding year, completed an approved driver education course. In this section, "completed" means the student participated in at least the required number of hours of instruction as required in s. PI 21.04(1).

(3) Aids shall be paid for the following categories of eligible students:

(a) During the school year, students enrolled in a high school.

(b) During the summer program, any person not over 19 years of age.

(4) During a cooperative program between a public and a private high school in which the private high school offers either the classroom or laboratory phase of the total program and the public high school offers the other instructional phase of the total program, the aids shall be paid to the public school district.

(5) School districts and CHCEBs applying for this aid shall report annually the number of students successfully completing the approved driver education course and other detailed information, including expenditures for salaries, equipment, and supplies for the course, on the annual report to the state superintendent.

Note: Form PI-1505 School district annual report, required by s. 120.18, Stats., of Form PI-1550 CHCEB annual report, authorized by s. 115.28(13), Stats.

(6) Aids shall be paid for programs taught in part by a public high school and in part by a VTAE school. Such programs shall be established by action of both the board of

education of the district operating the high school and the local VTAE board which are involved. Each board shall be responsible for that portion of the program taught as a part of its curriculum. However, the entire program shall be reported for approval by the public school district and aid shall be claimed by and paid to the public school district. Any distribution of the aid may be made locally as agreed upon between the respective boards. The responsibility for distributing the aid to the respective districts shall be specified in the action establishing the cooperative program.

(7) Aids paid for programs taught by a CESA under an agreement between a CESA and a public school district shall be claimed by and paid to the public school district. Aids may be paid only if the instructors are licensed as required by s. PI 21.04(3) and are CESA or school district employees.

(8) Aids shall be paid to VTAEs for programs which are approved by the board of vocational, technical and adult education under s. 343.06(1)(c), Stats.

History: Cr. Register, May, 1986, No. 365, eff. 7-1-86.

Appendix B

PI 3.13 of the Wisconsin Administrative Code

PI 3.13 Driver education – 450. A regular license or renewal of a regular license to teach driver and traffic safety education may be issued to an applicant who has completed or possesses all of the following:

(1) A Wisconsin teaching license;

(2) At least 3 years driving experience while holding a valid driver's license;

(3) A state's driver's license;

(4) An acceptable driving record;

(5) At least 15 semester credits of approved course work in driver and traffic safety education. At least 9 semester credits of the 15 semester credits shall include all of the following:

(a) A basic driver education course.

(b) An advanced driver education course.

(c) A general safety course.

(d) At least 3 semester credits of the 9 semester credits shall be in driver education which includes at least 10 class periods of experience in teaching practice driving.

(e) At least 6 semester credits of the 15 semester credits shall include specific courses in driver and traffic safety education that place emphasis upon critical factors that influence driver behavior in the driving task, including course work which develops teacher competencies in alcohol education and sociological and psychological behavior factors related to traffic safety.

History: Cr. Register, April, 1988, No. 388, eff. 5-1-88.

Appendix C
Resources

American Automobile Association (AAA)
1000 AAA Dr.
Heathrow, FL 32746-5063
(407) 444-7963

AAA Foundation for Traffic Safety
1440 New York Ave., N.W., Ste. 201
Washington, DC 20005
(202) 638-5944
(202) 638-5943 (Fax)

AIMS Media
9710 Desota
Chatsworth, CA 91311
1 (800) 367-2476

American Driver and Traffic Safety Education
  Association (ADTSEA)
Highway Safety Center
Indiana University of Pennsylvania
Indiana, PA 15705-1092
(412) 357-4051

ARCO
Public Affairs, Rm. 4473
515 S. Flower St.
Los Angeles, CA 90071
(213) 486-3384

Center for Unlimited Vision
80 Fifth Ave., Ste. 1105
New York, NY 10011
(212) 255-2240

Ford Motor Company
Fairlane Plaza South, Ste. 500
330 Town Center Dr.
Dearborn, MI 48126
(313) 845-8301

Foundation of Wisconsin Automobile and
  Truck Dealers
150 E. Gilman St., Ste. A
Madison, WI 53705
(608) 251-5577
(608) 251-4379 (Fax)

GEICO Insurance
1 GEICO Plaza
Washington, DC 20076

General Motors Corporation
3044 W. Grand Blvd.
Detroit, MI 48202
(313) 556-3623

General Motors Corporation
Driver Education Headquarters
P.O. Box 428
Birmingham, MI 48012-0428
1 (800) 932-2062

Glencoe Division
Macmillan/McGraw Hill
936 Eastwind Dr.
Westerville, OH 43081

In Motion magazine
General Learning Corporation
60 Revere Dr.
Northbrook, IL 60062-1563
(708) 205-3000

Insurance Institute for Highway Safety
Communications Department
1005 N. Glebe Rd.
Arlington, VA 02201
(703) 247-1500

Interactive Driving Systems, Inc.
P.O. Box 98
Cheshire, CT 06410
1 (800) 764-7767

Janus Interactive
1600 N.W. 167th Pl., Ste. 320
Beaverton, OR 97006
1 (800) 629-0835 or (503) 629-0587

Learning Corporation of America
420 Academy Dr.
Northbrook, IL 60062
(312) 940-1290

Lothair, Inc.
1132 S. Lothair Ave.
Chicago, IL 60643
(312) 239-8154

MADD, National Headquarters
511 E. John Carpenter Fwy., Ste. 700
Irving, TX 75062

MADD, Wisconsin Office
121 S. Main St., P.O. Box 28
Fond du Lac, WI 54936-0028
1 (800) 799-MADD or (414) 929-8485
(414) 929-8515 (Fax)

Manocherian Foundation, Inc.
3 New York Plaza, 18th Fl.
New York, NY 10004
(212) 837-4844

Miles Media
2124 F St.
Bakersfield, CA 93301
(805) 324-1665

Milwaukee Safety Commission
Safety Academy
6680 N. Teutonia Ave.
Milwaukee, WI 53209
(414) 935-7994
(414) 935-7924 (Fax)

Motorcycle Safety Foundation
2 Jennifer St., Ste. 150
Irvine, CA 92718
(714) 727-3227

National Highway Traffic Safety
    Administration
Office of Safety Programs
NTS-21
400 Seventh St., S.W.
Washington, DC 20590

National Highway Traffic Safety
    Administration
Office of Youth Programs
NTS-21
400 Seventh St., S.W.
Washington, DC 20590
(202) 366-2705
http://www.nhtsa.dot.gov/

National Safety Council
1121 Spring Lake Dr.
Itasca, IL 60143
(708) 775-2014
http://www.nsc.org/nsc/

National Student Safety Program
Highway Safety Center
Indiana University of Pennsylvania
Indiana, PA 15705-1092
(412) 357-4051

Office of the Commissioner of Insurance
121 E. Wilson St., P.O. Box 7873
Madison, WI 53707-7873
(608) 266-3585
(608) 266-9335 (Fax)

Operation Lifesaver, Inc.
1420 King St., Ste. 401
Alexandria, VA 22314

PDE Publications, Inc.
Traffic Safety Information Village
http://www.pde.drivers.com/pde/world.html

Physicians for Auto Safety
12 Church St.
New Melford, CT 06776
(203) 355-0323

Propulsion International, Inc.
3800 Isabelle, Ste. C
Brossard, Quebec, Canada
J4Y 2R3
(514) 444-7000

SADD, National Office
P.O. Box 800
Marlboro, MA 01752
(508) 481-3568
(508) 481-5759 (Fax)

SADD, Wisconsin Coordinator
Alcohol Traffic Safety Program
c/o Wisconsin Department of Public Instruction
125 S. Webster St., P.O. Box 7841
Madison, WI 53707-7841
(608) 266-9677

Safety Enterprises
1010 S. Summit
Bloomington, IL 61701
(309) 828-0906

Safety Industries
P.O. Box 1137
McGill, NV 89218-9900
(702) 235-7766

State Farm Insurance Company
1 State Farm Plaza
Bloomington, IL 61710

Think First Foundation
22 S. Washington St.
Park Ridge, IL 60068
(708) 692-2740

Tire Industry Safety Council
P.O. Box 1801
Washington, DC 20013

U.S. Department of Transportation
NHTSA
400 Seventh St., S.W.
Washington, DC 20590
(202) 366-2727
http://www.dot.gov/

Wisconsin AAA Association
8030 Excelsior Dr., P.O. Box 33
Madison, WI 53717-1939
1 (800) 426-5411 or (608) 836-6555
(608) 828-2443 (Fax)

Wisconsin Association of Wo/Mens Highway
　Safety Leaders
West 8294, Hwy. M
Merrill, WI 54452

Wisconsin Automobile and Truck Dealers
　Association
150 E. Gilman St., Ste. A
Madison, WI 53705
(608) 251-5577
(608) 251-4379 (Fax)

Wisconsin Council of Safety
A Division of the WMC Foundation, Inc.
P.O. Box 352
Madison, WI 53701-0352

Wisconsin Department of Public Instruction
Alcohol Traffic Safety Program
SSPW Team, 4th Fl.
125 S. Webster St., P.O. Box 7841
Madison, WI 53707-7841
(608) 266-9677
http://badger.state.wi.us/O/agencies/dpi/www/
　dpi_home.html

Wisconsin Department of Transportation
Bureau for Field Services
P.O. Box 8917
4802 Sheboygan Ave., Rm. 266
Madison, WI 53708-8917
(608) 266-0428
(608) 266-6750 (Fax)
http://www.dot.state.wi.us/

Wisconsin Department of Transportation
Maps and Publications Sales
3617 Pierstorff St., P.O. Box 7713
Madison, WI 53707-7713
(608) 246-3265
(608) 246-5632 (Fax)

Wisconsin Department of Transportation
Bureau of Transportation Safety
Rm. 809
4802 Sheboygan Ave.
Madison, WI 53708

Wisconsin Driver and Traffic Safety Education
　Association (WDTSEA)
Bob Garnett, WDTSEA Business Manager
c/o Adams–Friendship High School
420 N. Main St., P.O. Box 346
Adams, WI 53190-0346
(608) 339-3921

Current Textbooks (title and publisher)

Drive Right
Scott Forseman Company
1900 E. Lake Ave.
Glenview, IL 60025

Responsible Driving
Glencoe Order Department
P.O. Box 543
Blacklick, OH 43004-0543

Tomorrow's Drivers
Houghton Mifflin Company
One Beacon St.
Boston, MA 02108

Sportsmanlike Driving
c/o AAA
Traffic Safety and Engineering
1000 AAA Dr.
Heathrow, FL 32746-5063
(407) 444-7000

Simulation Resources

DORON Precision Systems, Inc.
P.O. Box 400
Binghamton, NY

Simulation Systems International
11130 E. 56th St.
Tulsa, OK 74146
1 (800) 843-4764

Traffic Crash Data Publications

- National Resources
— *Accident Facts*, from the National Safety Council
— *FARS* (Fatal Accident Reporting Systems), from NHTSA
- Wisconsin Resources
— *Wisconsin Crash Facts*, from the WDOT
— *Wisconsin Alcohol Crash Facts*, from the WDOT

Traffic Safety Education-Related Computer Software Resources

American Automobile Association (AAA)
Traffic Safety and Engineering
1000 AAA Dr.
Heathrow, FL 32746-5063
(407) 444-7000

Glencoe Publishing
Order Department
P.O. Box 543
Blacklick, OH 43004-0543

Houghton Mifflin Company
One Beacon St.
Boston, MA 02108

Janus Interactive
1600 N.W. 167th Pl., Ste. 320
Beaverton, OR 97006
1 (800) 629-0835 or (503) 629-0587

P.C. Games
P.O. Box 7624
Olympia, WA 98507
1 (800) 236-1300 or (206) 754-6095

Safety Industries
P.O. Box 1137
McGill, NV 89318-9900
(702) 235-7766
(702) 235-7767 (Fax)

Scott Forseman Company
1900 E. Lake Ave.
Glenview, IL 60025